British Railways in Unseen Colour: 1948-1962

Images from the Roy E. Vincent Archive
at the Transport Treasury

ABOVE 'B1' No 61399, possibly almost brand new, is photographed in early British Railways days. Constructed by the North British Locomotive Company, this engine was officially completed on 22 April 1952 and initially allocated to Doncaster. The design dated back ten years to 1942 when the first of the type were introduced, with 410 eventually built, 136 of them after nationalisation and the last in 1952. (A maximum of 409 were only ever in service as one, No 61057, was scrapped in 1950 consequent upon collision damage.) Two of the type are preserved, Nos 61264 and 61306, formerly LNER Nos 1264 and 1306 respectively. It has oft been the habit of only considering many of the BR Standard type steam engines as having had a short operational life, but No 61399, built in the 1950s, would suffer a similar fate as it was withdrawn from Canklow shed (Rotherham) in September 1963 and scrapped by Messrs Marples & Gillot of Sheffield early in 1964, one of five of the class to succumb there.

OPPOSITE 'Power and Majesty' – how could anyone not fail to be impressed by this low-angle image of the 'Royal Scot' headboard on No 46227 *Duchess of Devonshire*, taken at Carlisle on 23 April 1957? The train 'The Royal Scot' operated in both directions between Euston and Glasgow, and according to period either with a crew change or locomotive and crew change at Carlisle. For most of the time the service operated non-stop between London and Carlisle and was limited to eight coaches with standing passengers not permitted. The journey time for the complete journey behind steam was 7hr 15 min, compared with today's 4½-hour electric schedule. At the time of the photograph the engine was allocated to Glasgow, so when photographed may either have just come off the up working or be waiting for the down train.

British Railways in Unseen Colour: 1948-1962

Images from the Roy E. Vincent Archive
at the Transport Treasury

Compiled by Kevin Robertson

crecy.co.uk

First published in 2018 by Crécy Publishing

Reprinted in 2020 with revisions

All rights reserved. No part of this book may be reproduced or transmitted in any form or by any means electronic or mechanical, including photocopying, recording or by any information storage without permission from the Publisher in writing. All enquiries should be directed to the Publisher.

© Text Kevin Robertson 2018
　Images The R E Vincent collection at The Transport Treasury

A CIP record for this book is available from the British Library

Printed in Bulgaria by Multiprint

ISBN 978 1 90932 883 9

Crécy Publishing Limited
1a Ringway Trading Estate, Shadowmoss Road, Manchester M22 5LH
www.crecy.co.uk

FRONT COVER Steam engines come in all shapes and sizes, from the mighty and the magnificent to the seemingly small and insignificant. Each, though, was built with a specific purpose in mind and, even though superseded by a more modern replacement at some point, the old might still be found paying its way and serving its masters or perhaps even a new owner. Here is one covering all those criteria, dating back to the latter years of the 19th century and yet still active sixty years later and likely not far from its original haunts. The location is the BR steam depot at Carlisle Kingmoor and the engine, No 57340, a Drummond 0-6-0 built for the Caledonian Railway and introduced from 1883 onwards. In its 60-plus years of life so far it will have travelled many miles and pulled literally thousands of tons, unsung and ignored by many, but a true workhorse of the rails. We may even ponder at the number of times those wheels have turned, how many times the whistle has screeched and how many tons of coal have been shovelled by man to feed the furnace within. Time, though, has taken its toll: the vacuum pipe running along the outside of the framing is loose at the front end, while the boiler handrail has also taken a bashing. Are the footplatemen nearby putting off the time when they will have to work this engine on their next turn, or simply keeping out of the way of the camera? Whatever, No 57340 would soldier on a while longer, finishing its life at the end of 1962, having given seventy years of service.

BACK COVER MAIN A panoramic view of Bangor station on 27 July 1955 with at least five steam engines and a diesel multiple unit visible. The station is at its infrastructure peak, with four platforms plus a bay.

INSET CLOCKWISE FROM TOP

The Great Western branch line is represented here by '45xx' No 4552 and a short freight at Moorswater on 18 July 1960.

This panoramic view of Inverness features a southbound service for Perth and beyond leaving behind a pair of 'Black 5s'.

This is the delightfully rural location of Penmaenpool (between Barmouth and Bala Junction) and its locomotive shed.

Here is an example of a small Southern engine in the shape of former SECR 'P' Class 0-6-0T No 31325 seen at Brighton on 30 March 1957.

Seemingly fresh from the paint shop, LNER 'B17' No 61661 is depicted at Marylebone on 6 April 1949.

A view of the train shed in Callington; as with the locomotive depot, it comprises corrugated sheeting over a timber frame.

Contents

Introduction..6

The Archive..7

Index of locomotive types and locations...................................206

Introduction

Roy was born 1920 in Stratford, east London, and attended the Central Foundation Boys School in City Road near Liverpool Street station. Following school he worked for the LNER as a clerk – his training being as an accountant – but at the beginning of the Second World War Roy moved to Newquay in Cornwall to avoid the Blitz. He then joined the Army and was posted to the REME. Roy served in Persia and later in Italy, notably being left behind by his unit when wrongly diagnosed with a heart condition and hospitalised against his will!

Once the war ended he returned to work with the LNER, then British Railways, where he was able to us his access to railway property to carry on his photographic interests with some success. He served his final years at York's railway headquarters as an Establishment Officer, having moved from accounts to the personnel side of the job. Roy retired from British Railways in 1975.

Once retired he worked on slide tape productions and acted as a consultant for Saville Photographic in York. Unfortunately, he was diagnosed with lung cancer in 1980 and died in October of that year.

His legacy is one of the few glimpses of colour on Britain's railways in the years after 1947. Unfortunately his listing does not appear to include all the images taken, and even when this was the case sometimes dates and even location details have to be omitted. Similarly there are gaps, the years 1950 through to 1953 having little if any coverage. (If anyone can add further detail, particular locations, etc, do please get in touch so any necessary additions can be made for future editions.)

The name Roy Vincent may perhaps not be familiar to all students or enthusiasts of railways, but it certainly should be. An early exponent of colour photography, Roy was active in this medium from around 1947 onwards, a time when colour was very much in its infancy; indeed, even the private use of black and white film was nowhere near as prolific as would be the case later.

But ignoring the gaps, what we have is a fascinating collection of photographs from the period – a time of transition when steam was on the one hand still supreme, yet moves were afoot to effect change. It was a time through which many of those to whom this book is aimed will have lived, but perhaps like me only witnessed a very small portion thereof, so here is the opportunity to redress that balance.

It should be explained that the master list of Roy's images is not in date or loco order. Neither does it cover all the images. Consequently we have deliberately included the views in random order with no attempt to categorise regions, locomotive types or subjects. As such there should be a surprise on every page – well, that is the intention!

Considering also that some of the slides seen are fast approaching 70 years of age, and subject to the vagaries of some of the colour film from the period, the condition of the vast majority is excellent. The odd one has been excluded for reasons of quality or duplicity, but we do ask for indulgence where some colours may not perhaps have survived as well as others. None have been 'colourised' or started their life other than as colour views.

I would like to express gratitude to the Transport Treasury and in particular Robin Fell and Barry Hoper, and also to Kevin Potts for assistance in making the selection. In providing caption information, whenever possible reference has been made to Roy's original notes, as well as numerous emails to my long-term friend Amyas Crump, together with reference to literally hundreds of books, magazines and websites. (I had almost forgotten the colour of the carpet in the office!) Any errors I will claim full credit for.

Kevin Robertson, 2018

I would like to thank those who have kindly written in to put right my 'senior moments' of which a few slipped past the several times the text was read though. The names I have are W Clark, Stuart Hicks, David Letcher, and Garry Thorp, but there are at least two others as well whose comments arrived without annotation. Gentleman/ladies, I thank you all.

Kevin Robertson, 2020

(Note – copies of images from this book will be available from the Transport Treasury shortly. They may only be obtained from this source and are not available from the publisher or author.)

The Archive

We start this photographic journey with 'Castle' Class 4-6-0 No 5049 *Earl of Plymouth* appropriately at Plymouth Laira and carrying 'The Cornishman' headboard and train identification number '675'. Originating in broad-gauge days – just – a train of that name first ran in the summer of 1890 between London and Cornwall and was unusual for a fast train of the period in that it carried 3rd Class passengers. Indeed, the down service of 20 May 1892 was immortalised as being the final broad-gauge express to leave Paddington prior to the conversion of the broad gauge to standard or, as the Great Western would have it, 'narrow' gauge. The 'Cornishman' name was modified to that of the 'Cornish Riviera Express' in July 1904, but revitalised again as a separate service in 1935 as a relief to the 'Limited', as the 'Cornish Riviera Express' had by then become known. At the time it was to be but a brief return, for in the summer timetable the train had returned to anonymity. A penchant for naming trains returned in the early 1950s and British Railways reintroduced the 'Cornishman' name, but this time for a service between the Midlands and Cornwall, the actual Midlands area routing varying over the years. Even in the early 1970s the service could still be identified by name with the northern destinations of Leeds and Bradford. Come the early 21st century and the wheel has literally turned full circle with 'The Cornishman' as a named service once more running between London Paddington and Plymouth, although no longer of course behind engines of the 'Castle' Class.

A close-up of the headboard reveals a pixie surmounting a toadstool. No 5049 was built at Swindon in May 1936 and originally carried the name *Denbigh Castle*. It was renamed just over a year later in August 1937, and is seen here with four-row superheater and Hawksworth tender, but yet to receive its final modification, a double chimney. The allocation is shown as '83D', meaning Plymouth Laira. British Railways introduced number and letter codes to identify locomotive allocations after 1948; it was based on LMS practice but meant the attaching of a small oval plate to the smokebox door of every steam engine. (Well, 99% probably, as some engines, although allocated a depot, were withdrawn before it could be attached.) Previously in Great Western days a two- or three-letter code had been stencilled on to the engine frame immediately behind the buffer beam, examples being 'OOC' for Old Oak Common, 'RDG' for Reading and 'LA' for Laira.

Class 4 tank No 80110 is seen at Kittybrewster shed, Aberdeen, on 20 April 1957. It is a BR Standard Class 4 tank, a design almost universally liked and one that could equally be seen on most regions of British Railways with the exception of the Western. It displays the typical Scottish Region red background to its name and shed plate as well as white-painted buffers – a recent special working perhaps? – as well as a small snowplough and additional three-link wagon coupling. Twelve engines of the class were allocated to the depot over the years. The shed itself had both a roundhouse and a straight-road shed and was operational between 1854 and 1961. After the latter date it spent a period as a repository for stored – surplus to requirements – steam engines, including for a while various members of the 'A4' Class. The site was subsequently cleared and there is now nothing to indicate its former use. Following the depot closure No 80110 still had some useful life left and was transferred, but was finally withdrawn for scrap from 66A, Polmadie shed in Glasgow, on 8 May 1965, having been operational for just 10½ years.

Roy's images were not restricted just to steam, as witness here No D601 *Ark Royal*, one of five members of the 'Warship' Class named after Royal Navy vessels and of the diesel-hydraulic type. (Perhaps the names were chosen as the engines were anticipated to be working trains to Plymouth, where of course the Navy maintained a sizeable presence.) Introduced in 1957/58 as the first main-line diesel class on the Western Region, it is claimed on the internet – https://en.wikipedia.org/wiki/British_Rail_Class_41_(Warship_Class) – that the type was not actually wanted by the WR, which was instead keen on the D800 type due to enter service shortly afterwards. The British Transport Commission, however, was insistent and saw the design as being able to effect a direct comparison with the English Electric Type 4 (D200) series diesel-electric version.

Viewed very much as the start of modernisation on the WR, it must be admitted that the type was successful, although as more and more of the D800 series – also a diesel-hydraulic design – came on stream the D600s were banished further west and ended up being used mainly between Penzance and Plymouth. Being a small class and consequently non-standard, they were an early casualty for withdrawal and all ceased work en bloc on 30 December 1967. One survived at the Woodham Brothers scrapyard at Barry until 1980, but at the time was considered unsuitable for preservation. It is perhaps ironic that not only did No D600 spent more time in a scrapyard than it ever had in service, but it also spent that time surrounded by the very steam engines it had been intended to replace. The view was taken at Plymouth in June 1958 with a 'Modernisation' sign for North Road station in the background during the period that the class was working the 'Cornish Riviera Express', complete with steam-design headboard!

Roy's photographs were not confined to locomotives either, as seen here with former Pullman 'Mauchline Belle' devoid of name and Pullman livery and instead carrying the identification 'SC218M'. This vehicle started life in 1913 as a K-type all-1st Class car, one of three built by Clayton Wagons in Lincoln. 'Mauchline Belle' was one of three identical Pullman cars each named after historical or fictional Scottish heroines, intended to be used as luxury accommodation on what were the former Caledonian routes of what was by then the LMS. The contract between Pullman and the LMS came to an end in 1933 and, having failed in an attempt to find further Pullman work, 'Mauchline Belle' was part of a batch sold to the LMS, which immediately painted out the 'Pullman' designation and name and used the vehicles as restaurant cars – latterly unclassed. In that guise this vehicle continued in service until withdrawn in April 1961. It is seen here at Inverness on 19 April 1957, with a horse box nearby. No SC218M remained in the Scottish area for most if not all of its operational life.

'Britannia' No 70037 *Hereward the Wake* stands at Cambridge on 24 July 1955. One of a number of the class allocated to the former GER lines of the Eastern Region, the engines revolutionised fast train working in and out of Liverpool Street and would continue to do until ousted by electrification. No 70037 is seen is sparkling condition – even the handrails on the smoke deflectors and across the smokebox are polished. Allocated first to Stratford when new from Crewe in December 1952, it later moved to Norwich Thorpe, followed by the depots at March and Immingham before being transferred to the London Midland Region in November 1963. Its final years saw it based around Carlisle, and it was withdrawn from the city's Kingmoor shed in early November 1966 before being sold for scrap to J. McWilliams of Shettlestone, Glasgow, less than four weeks after ceasing work, one of nineteen members of the class of 55 'Britannias' that would end their days in the same scrapyard.

Sparkling 'M7' 0-4-4T No 30036 pokes its front out of the shed at Plymouth Friary into the sunshine on 15 April 1956. The smokebox shows evidence of some hard work in the past, but I think that can be excused considering that the engine was just coming up to its 58th birthday. It is a standard version of the type, not fitted for push-pull working (which would be indicated by additional pipework at the front). Friary had an allocation of around twenty steam engines, mostly tank engines but also some 4-4-0s for passenger services to and from Exeter. Lucas Terrace Halt on the Plymstock branch was located hard by the east end of the site. No 30036 was at work until January 1964, by which time it had transferred its allegiance to Bournemouth.

A somewhat weary and work-stained No 6870 *Bodicote Grange* is recorded at Plymouth Laira in May 1960. The depot here consisted of both a roundhouse – in the background – and a four-road straight shed – out of sight to the left. No 6870 appears to be in use for depot shunting, an unusual task perhaps for an engine of this type, but it may simply have been all that was available, or perhaps it was confined to light duties. At the time No 6870 was just 21 years of age and had a further five years of life. Like all other members of the eighty-strong class, it succumbed to scrap but great strides are being made by the Betton Grange Society to effect a 'new-build' using as many standard Swindon parts as possible.

Portrait of a 'King': No 6008 runs light engine at Plymouth with Laira depot in the background, the purpose probably being to turn the engine to face the opposite direction using the triangle whose arms were Laira Junction to the east, Lipsom Junction to the west, and Mount Gould Junction to the south – No 6008 is seen between the last two named. It will be seen that the engine has a tender full of coal, so is likely being turned prior to reversing back to North Road for an up express. No date is recorded but we can say for certain it is pre-1955 when double chimneys were fitted to the class. The 'Kings' slowly migrated away from work on Plymouth to Paddington trains as the diesel-hydraulics took over, instead finding new work on South Wales trains via the Severn Tunnel, a route on which they were previously banned. Their final workings were on the Birmingham trains, although even on these there was competition from the Blue Pullman diesel sets introduced in 1960. Three members of the thirty-strong class are preserved, but No 6008 is not one of them.

The only photograph of a 'Princess' in the collection shows No 46207 *Princess Arthur of Connaught* in store at Camden on an unreported date. Built at Crewe in 1935, the twelve members of the class remained in front-line service, latterly on Liverpool services, until ousted by diesel traction from the late 1950s onwards. The end would come not long after this, and No 46207 ended its days at Willesden in 1961. The storage of steam locomotives was commonplace throughout the railways in the 1950s, usually due to fluctuations in traffic. Even the most powerful machines would find themselves draped with cloths and the chimney tied over as here; after all, why steam No 46207 for perhaps menial work when a smaller engine could undertake the same task using a lot less fuel? Considering its excellent external condition it is quite possible that No 46207 would be once again in service at a later date.

Included in the collection are several views of non-BR or British narrow-gauge topics, some examples of which we have included. Here at Neasden on 1 June 1957 is one of the twenty electric locomotives built in 1923 for the Metropolitan Railway and intended for service on the outer-London electric service to Chesham/Amersham and Aylesbury. No 2 was originally named *Oliver Cromwell* but was renamed *Thomas Lord* in 1953, after the man who gave the land for what became known as Lord's cricket ground. (Thomas Lord is buried at West Meon in Hampshire, where his name also survives at the local hostelry. The nameplate carried by No 2 also featured a plaque and crossed cricket bats.)

The class was released from passenger duty following the introduction of 'A' stock electric multiple units, and most of the survivors apart from Nos 1, 3, 5 and 12 were withdrawn. (No 15 had been withdrawn in 1951.) The remaining four were then used for departmental duties, although this was not to be for long as three were withdrawn in 1963, leaving No 5 (from the first batch of withdrawals preserved at the London Transport Museum), and No 12 retained for brake-block testing and occasional special train use. (No 12 has been modified to work on both three- and four-rail electrified systems.) No 2 was one of four sent for scrap at Rugby in March 1962, although it is possible that it may still have been extant as much as three years later. The identity of the class member behind is not reported.

This panoramic view shows the former Midland Railway line and engine shed at Upper Bank, Swansea, on the original Swansea Vale Railway, recorded on 17 April 1955. Originally part of the Swansea Vale Railway connecting the industries and coalfields along the River Tawe with Swansea, the route here had commenced life as a tramroad in 1846, then a goods-only railway and eventually a passenger-carrying line from 1860. With plenty of goods traffic, the railway was profitable but even so was always short of capital, hence the involvement of the MR, first in 1874 as lessee, then from 1876 as purchaser. The route ran north-east from Swansea through Upper Bank where there was a western loop though Morrison, and on to Glais, Pontardawe and Ynysygeinon. At the latter point the line split again, one part joining the Neath & Brecon and the other heading towards a connection with the Llanelly Railway at Brynamman.

Opened in 1871, the station at Upper Bank had already been closed to passengers for five years when this photograph was taken in 1955, although goods continued to be handled until the next decade. The 1950s had also seen a decline in the traditional anthracite mines and smelting works that the route had once served, and by 1973 the final section north from Swansea through Upper Bank as far as Llansamlet ceased operation. The railway then remained moribund for almost a decade until formal closure in September 1982.

It's the end of the road for former Great Eastern 'T26' (reclassified 'E4' by the LNER) 2-4-0 No 62788 on the scrap line at Stratford on 30 March 1958 and still formally allocated to Cambridge. It was officially withdrawn the following day, although had probably not worked for some time. One hundred of the type were produced by James Holden at the Stratford Works of the GER between 1891 and 1902 and found gainful employment on passenger trains into Norfolk as well as the movement of horse boxes to Newmarket. After 1923 heavier trains demanded larger engines and the type was relegated to secondary and branch use. Eighteen were taken over by British Railways at nationalisation but their numbers continued to dwindle and the last was withdrawn in 1959; incidentally, they were also the last 2-4-0 tender engines at work in Britain. One, No 62785 – GER No 490 – has been preserved. No 62788, GER No 496/LNER No 7496/7805/2788, was finally disposed of where it had been built, at Stratford.

At the end of the month following that when No 62788 was seen awaiting its fate, its sister engine, the now preserved No 62785, was photographed on 27 April 1958 at Haverhill with a 'CURC' (Cambridge University Railway Society) special. The train left Cambridge around 9.30am and went to and fro between Bartlow and Haverhill with two CURS members sharing the driving and firing under the supervision of a driver and inspector. This was possible as there were no Sunday trains on the line until much later in the day. The line between Shelford, south of Cambridge, and Sudbury was closed to passengers on 6 March 1967, Haverhill having been the last station to retain goods until the last day of 1966. Despite diesel multiple units (DMUs) and railbuses being introduced, they failed to stem the tide away from rail although in recent years there has been some hope that the route may eventually reopen. Scenes such as this on a rural railway were once commonplace, the whole giving the impression of a quieter and somehow less 'clinical' world. Small wonder it is also often the scenario the heritage routes as well as the railway modelling fraternity seek to recreate.

The same train pauses at Haverhill Junction signal box with the signalman in conversation with the driver. The 'junction' here referred to the connection with the Colne Valley & Halstead Railway, which had lost its passenger service in 1961 and freight in 1965. (A short section of the route has since reopened as a heritage line.) No 62785 can be seen to have been fitted with a tender cab, while the class designation 'E4' is also written in white on the buffer beam. Likely the 'A' lamp code – for an express passenger service – was a bit of 'University licence'! The engine is certainly smartly turned out for the special with polished brass to the clack valve, surrounding the front spectacle plate and splasher and also on the cover to the bearing of the front wheel.

On the left the tall signal has a concrete post. These type of posts were first seen on the Midland & Great Northern system, having been introduced by its engineer William Marriott. The design was later taken up by the LNER as a cheaper option than timber, while elsewhere the GWR also used concrete for a period, possibly when timber was in short supply. Despite perhaps their obvious advantage, the biggest difficulty was in moving a completed post from the horizontal, in which position it had been cast, to the vertical. Stress introduced during this operation could easily result in cracks, which would subsequently let in moisture, leading to freezing and the concrete starting to 'blow'. No 62785 is another engine shown with a '31A' Cambridge allocation.

'45xx' No 4549 leaves Mary Tavy & Blackdown station with a southbound train from Launceston to Yelverton and Plymouth. The date is not recorded but it is interesting to note that the engine has not yet received its BR smokebox number and the Great Western practice of a painted number on the buffer beam still persists. This station was located about half a mile from both the villages in its name, and was originally just known as Mary Tavy – the extra designation was added in 1907. A passing loop had originally been provided, hence also the signal box, but the loop was removed as far back as 1892, while further economy occurred half a century later when after 11 August 1941 goods also ceased to be handled – not that there was likely to be much. Slightly to the east of the station was the main Southern line between Plymouth and Okehampton, and while each company had its own stations at Tavistock to the south and Launceston to the north, in this area the GWR served the location; the Southern had its own stopping place, named Brentor. Perhaps not surprisingly a quiet location such as this could hardly have contributed much to its own upkeep let alone the main network, and the railway was closed in 1962. No 4549 is unlikely to have collected or indeed deposited any fare-paying passengers during its brief pause.

BELOW This freshly repainted signal is the up starting signal at Saltash in May 1959, with the bridge of the same name in the distance behind. It is a standard GWR wooden post with 4-foot arms, and the distant is fixed. Note the tubing protecting the operating wire that runs up the side of the post. Not visible, although there would have to have been one, is the counterweight to the operating lever raised high on the post; this was common practice when signals had of necessity to be placed on a station platform, and was thus designed to prevent injury to staff and passengers. The lamp and possibly also the position of the arm are electrically repeated in the signal box – hence the electrical connection and terminal box – while there would also appear to be a telephone in the box on the far side of the post. The shadow is caused by the platform canopy.

ABOVE An unusual livery for 'Jubilee' class 4-6-0 No 45671 *Prince Rupert* at Crewe on 19 March 1960. The engine is fresh from mechanical overhaul and will probably have been moved outside for a steam test before visiting the paint shop. Even so, the artisans from that particular location have already done some work as the loco displays an unusual pink undercoat. Beyond is Fairburn-design 2-6-4T No 42674, and further back still is an Ivatt 2-6-2T. This could well have been No 45671's last major works overhaul, as it was withdrawn from traffic on 9 November 1963 and subsequently cut up, again at Crewe, just one of the 3,368 engines to meet their end at the works.

Another ex-works locomotive is No 73054 at Swindon on 6 September 1959. Built at Derby in 1954, this was one of the class later allocated to Bath Green Park for services over the Somerset & Dorset line, where the class was well liked, especially on the prestige 'Pines Express' working. Swindon has out of habit presented the engine in lined green, while many of the class wore black, although the named examples working on the Southern Region were also green at first. The 'Standard 5' type was not a regular performer on the Western Region and it is likely that No 73054 has been dealt with at Swindon where at the time the works had spare capacity. Moving locomotives around the country for necessary works visits was a fairly regular occurrence; Eastleigh, for example, dealt with engines from the LMR in the mid-1960s. After a life of just over eleven years, No 73054 was withdrawn from traffic on 31 August 1965.

An LNER articulated electric set stands at Newcastle Central in September 1948. In 1937 the LNER updated and expanded the original North Eastern Railway suburban Tyneside electric system, sixty-four new train sets being provided, each an articulated twin-set. Originally having both 1st and 3rd class accommodation, this was to be abolished some years later in 1959. The striking blue and off-white livery – well, certainly striking when fresh and clean – had been introduced in 1941, perhaps a slightly surprising time considering the pressures of war that then existed. It also replaced an earlier red and cream livery. Notwithstanding all the sets being of just two vehicles, there were four differing types of seating accommodation designated as types 'A' to 'D': eighteen in the Motor 3rd/Trailer 3rd; sixteen in Luggage Motor 3rd/Trailer 1st; eighteen in Motor 3rd/Trailer 3rd (non-driving), and eighteen in Luggage Motor 3rd/Trailer 1st (non driving – respectively). Types 'A' and 'B' were used as the two-coach sets when required, while types 'C' and 'D' were used to lengthen trains up to eight vehicles. The system was powered by the 600V DC third rail system. The sets were in operation until their being non-standard on what was an isolated system meant that they were no longer considered viable. This, coupled with declining traffic, meant that DMUs were considered a better option, and all the electric units had ceased work, replaced by diesels, by 11 June 1967.

Roy Vincent's photography was not solely confined to the main and branch lines, at times he would go 'off piste', as in August 1955 when he recorded Fowler diesel *Efficiency* at work at Marland on the 3-foot-gauge North Devon clay system. The Marland Light Railway was opened back in 1880 to convey clay from the works to what was then the nearest standard-gauge station at Torrington. Subsequently part of the route was incorporated into what became the standard-gauge North Devon & Cornwall Junction Light Railway, which opened in July 1925. The 3-foot line remained in operation in the area of the works until a system of internal roadways was completed and the railway system closed in 1970. Diesel traction took over from steam from 1947 onwards, the last steam engine being scrapped in March 1952. A total of seven four-wheel diesel-mechanical shunters were acquired between 1947 and 1965, two of them bearing the name *Efficiency*; that seen here was the first to bear the name and was built in 1951. It is believed that it remained on site until the end of rail use, although was likely not in use during the last years. On the extreme right is one of the doors of the two-road engine shed.

Another oddity, BR No 15098, was a petrol 0-4-0 built in 1919 for the Great Eastern Railway by the Motor Rail & Tram Car Company under its Simplex brand as Works No 1931. It became LNER No 8340, later 8188, then after nationalisation was given the number seen here. Although not confirmed, the view was likely taken at Stratford, with No 15098 proudly displaying 'R.A.1' ('Route Availability 1'), meaning that it could go basically anywhere. With a weight of just 8 tons, its hauling power would naturally be limited, so it would be restricted to light shunting. There were three in the class; the first was withdrawn in 1950 while No 15098 together with sister engine 15099 survived until 1956. The latter two are both reported to have been identified by BR numbers 68188 and 68199 respectively, although it is not confirmed that these were actually carried.

This image caused some head-scratching when attempting to confirm information – of course, like anything it's easy if you know! We have established that this machine was built for the Manchester, Bury, Rochdale and Oldham tramway, which opened an extensive steam-powered tramway covering a number of urban areas to the north and east of Manchester in 1883. Unfortunately it never reached Manchester, as that would have involved running over the existing horse tramways of the Manchester Carriage & Tramways Company and the necessary permission was not forthcoming. Nevertheless, for a time following the route's completion in 1884 the company operated the largest steam tramway undertaking in the world (at 33¼ miles).

This is No 84, one of four similar engines built by Beyer Peacock and numbered 83-86. The tramway experienced severe financial difficulties in 1886/87, but it appears that No 84 may have been working perhaps as late as May 1904. It was then used in industrial service until February 1954 – we have not been able to establish where – and was also sold to the Ince Forge at Wigan, where it was converted into a works shunter. It was at this stage that buffers were also fitted. Its life here was destined to be brief for at the end of September 1954 it was withdrawn and presented to the British Transport Commission for preservation. The engine was then stored at a variety of locations, including, as seen here, at Crewe, where it was photographed on 19 March 1960. Subsequently it has moved to at least two preservation sites and is currently in the custody of Crich museum but stored off-site. Restoration is a hoped-for but long-term project.

A beautifully clean Isle of Wight 'O2' 0-4-4T No W35 *Freshwater* enters the loop at Shanklin with a limited-stop Ryde to Ventnor train on 14 August 1964. Due to the position of the down siding, the position of the home signal had of necessity to be on the opposite side of the line, but bracketed so as to afford a clear view to the crew on their approach. No date is given but it is certainly summer, judging from the vegetation and more so from the number of droplights in the down position, indicating a warm day. No W35 was one of the final pair from the 'O2' Class to be transferred to the island as late as 1949. It was also in the final batch of withdrawals of the class when steam finished in 1967. The number '5' indicates the loco duty number from Ryde shed.

'A1/1' No 60113 *Great Northern* is a Thompson rebuild of an 'A10', identified by the unusual – to the eye, that is – position of the cylinders between the front driving wheel and bogie, and also the sloping smoke deflectors. Very much a 'one-off' by the designer, this engine was intended to be the prototype of a new class, improving on the work of Edward Thompson's predecessor Sir Nigel Gresley. In the event Thompson retired and the 'A1' Class as built by his successor Arthur Peppercorn was a vastly different machine.

When rebuilt in 1945, No 4470, as it was then, had been the very first Gresley 'Pacific' built and might rightly even have been considered for future preservation. Even among the LNER hierarchy there was debate as to whether this was a suitable engine to rebuild owing to its heritage, but Thompson was adamant and the work progressed. To this day there remains discussion as to whether the choice of this engine from among the members of what was then the 'A10' Class was right, some seeing it as a swipe at Gresley, with others feeling that the choice was right simply based on economics and which engine of the type was due for overhaul anyway. Whatever, there were teething problems with the rebuild that were eventually resolved, but for whatever reason No 60113 was never a regular performer on the fastest trains operating on the East Coast Main Line. Perhaps even those involved in day-to-day operation felt that to do so would have been a slur on the memory of Sir Nigel Gresley. The engine is seen here at King's Cross in May 1957; after a mediocre career in the form seen, No 60113 was retired in 1962 and scrapped.

A Kittybrewster-based locomotive recorded at Keith on 20 April 1957, 'K2/2' 2-6-0 No 61783 was one of a type first introduced onto the Great Northern Railway by Nigel Gresley (as he was then) in April 1914, and it is seen here in BR days with an unusual green background to its BR numberplate – a sign of respect perhaps to its former LNER green livery? The class originated from the similar 'K1' type, also designed by Gresley and introduced from 1912, of which ten were built. Modifications were then made to the design including a longer firebox, larger boiler and superheater, and longer frames. The pony truck was also moved forward slightly. Sixty-five engines were built to this new 'K2' designation in batches between 1914 and 1921, some by outside contractors; No 61783 was one of these, and originated from the firm of Kitson of Leeds. The original ten engines were subsequently rebuilt, and by 1937 the original 'K1' Class was extinct. Officially the rebuilt originals were Class 'K2/1' with 'K2/2' for the newer design. One change that did take place over the years was the provision of a side window to the cab; no doubt because of the climate, the cabs of those based in Scotland were not popular, and this side window cab was an appeasement. Indeed, locomotives that were subsequently moved to Scotland were similarly modified.

All seventy-five, including the rebuilt original ten, survived into BR days, thirteen carrying the names of Scottish lochs, these being the engines often seen working on the West Highland line to Fort William and Mallaig. No 61783 was one of them, and was named *Loch Shiel*. In June 1953 it was reported as still being in LNER Apple Green livery, no doubt somewhat weathered by that time. The LNER and indeed BR had intended that the type should be replaced on their duties by newer members of the 'B1' Class, and indeed this was the case, with the first of the design going for scrap in 1955. However, such was the decline of steam that some 'B1s' went for scrap before the 'K2s' they were intended to replace. No 61783 survived until 30 June 1959 working from the depot at Keith, and was disposed of exactly three months later, coincidentally also becoming the last of the class to be taken out of service, in 1962. None are preserved.

There are shades of the 1955 film *The Ladykillers* in this view of the comings and goings at Belle Isle outside King's Cross, likely in 1959. Three trains and engines are identified: nearest the camera is an 'A3' on a passenger working; next a Brush Type 2, also on front-line duty, as identified by the '1' prefix on the headcode; and finally 'A4' No 60028 seemingly stationary. Across the top runs the North London line, while leading to the right is the curve to King's Cross goods and St Pancras Junction on the North London. The whole is an impression of smoke, fumes and grime – and why not, for steam trains had been passing here for more than a hundred years and they were bound to leave their mark.

For those why might not have seen the original black comedy featuring Alec Guinness, *The Ladykillers* revolves around a gang of crooks who rent rooms in the house of an old lady living above the railway. Having stolen a considerable amount of money, each subsequently meets his end in a grisly way, the last knocked into the wagon of a passing train in consequence of being hit on the head by a signal arm.

LEFT Wheel and footplate detail of 'D16/3' 4-4-0 No 62613 were recorded at March on 28 May 1960, likely soon after overhaul or at the very least a good clean! Built at Stratford in June 1923, the type was used for many years on the former Great Eastern lines, hence the inclusion of the Westinghouse brake pump visible between the splashers. (Coaching stock on the GER was air-braked and a Westinghouse pump produced the compressed air.) Notice too the builder's plate. The 4-4-0 wheel arrangement was commonplace among most if not all of the major railway companies in the early years of the 20th century, although as train weights and speeds increased there came a need for an additional pair of wheels, giving rise to the 4-6-0 wheel arrangement. No 62613 was one of the type rebuilt by Gresley in 1938 with a round-top firebox replacing the original flat-top Belpaire example, thus changing its identity from LNER No 8782 to BR No 62613 in 1948, at that time being allocated to Yarmouth Beach (32F) depot. Withdrawal of the class started back in 1945, but No 62613 worked on until withdrawn from March depot on 31 October 1960, being disposed of exactly two months later as the last member of the class. (A side view of the full engine appears later.)

RIGHT Former LMS 0-6-0 diesel shunter No 7089, BR No 12012, entered service from Derby Works on 31 December 1939. It was one of thirty of the class based on a joint Stanier/English-Electric design with jack-shaft drive. The LMS had been one of the pioneers of the use of the diesel shunter and while the other companies had recognised its advantages it was the LMS that was the first to multiply what was then a standard design in larger quantities. This particular type was fitted with a single motor and the class would be developed further after the end of hostilities. Renumbered as seen from 12 February 1949 – it took some time to physically renumber all the locomotive, coaching and wagon stock after 1948 – this particular machine wandered widely during its BR days including spells (sometimes more than one) at Toton, Speke Junction, Crewe South, Monument Lane, Bescot, Bushbury and Oxley. Likely this was intended to gain experience on all types of work, other members of the class seeming to have also enjoyed wanderlust. Notwithstanding its usefulness, it was considered as non-standard once the BR 350hp shunter entered service in quantity, yet still achieved a useful life of just under thirty years before being broken up by W. Hatton Ltd at Bolton MPD in early July 1968. The photograph was taken at Crewe in July 1961.

Another early diesel type is represented by 204hp Drewry 0-6-0 No 11112 dating from 1952. Fifteen of the type were introduced, this particular example placed initially at Ipswich. They had a Gardner engine, fluid coupling and five-speed gearbox. Initially all the type were allocated to the Eastern Region and took over former steam duties at locations such as the Wisbech & Upwell Tramway (for which certain members of the class were fitted with side-skirting and cow-catchers), as well as Yarmouth Docks, the Ipswich Docks tramway and Parkeston Quay. From July 1959 No 11112 became BR No D2211, but the left the ER in 1966 and was reported as 'stored unserviceable' at, of all places, Feltham on the Southern Region by September 1966. It was transferred to the London Midland Region in May 1967, initially to Derby, where by 11 July 1970 it was reported as 'stored'. Reinstated a week later, it was likely then examined and found to be uneconomic or unsuitable to use for whatever reason and was withdrawn on 19 July. This time there would be no reprieve and it was cut up at Llanelli in November 1980. The class was extinct on BR by May 1972, but some had been sold to industry and four reported as exported to Italy around the same year. The engine is seen here at Stratford in September 1957. Notice too in the background a tantalising glimpse of withdrawn carriage stock.

British Railways in Unseen Colour: 1948-1962

THIS PAGE AND OPPOSITE On 23 June 1956 the Locomotive Club of Great Britain organised a special working over the Welshpool & Llanfair Railway using one of the two original locomotives, No 822 *The Earl*. The special train worked one complete round trip with passengers carried in a variety of goods stock – no 'health and safety', and no one seemed to mind. (Perhaps they might have objected had the weather been different.) Roy recorded several images, and we may assume that variations in the light/film are the reason why No 822 appears black on one side and green on the other! The attire of the visitors is of course another feature of sixty-plus years ago – raincoats, collars and ties all 'de rigueur' for the period. No 822 was one of a pair of small 0-6-0T engines built especially for the 2ft 6in-gauge line in 1902 by the firm of Beyer Peacock.

The railway opened in 1904 and, unlike other narrow-gauge lines in Wales whose purpose was the movement of minerals, the W&L was instead intended to provide a link from Welshpool to the community at Llanfair Caereinion, 8½ miles distant. The railway was operated by Cambrian Railways, but is reported never to have made a profit. Even so, it was absorbed, together with the other assets of the Cambrian company, into the Great Western in 1923, which continued to operate a passenger service until February 1931. Part of the reason for the poor receipts was the necessary engineering and cost of construction – the route abounded in sharp curves as well as climbing some 600 feet over its course, having first started from alongside the standard-gauge station at Welshpool. After 1931 No 822 and sister engine No 823 *Countess* continued working what was now a freight-only line. (There was a very temporary return to a passenger service for a few days in August 1945 in connection with the local Eisteddfod, the replacement bus service not being considered able to cope.) Freight continued for a further quarter century from 1931 until it too was withdrawn in November 1956. Both engines, however, officially remained 'on the books' until the early 1960s and were 'allocated' to Oswestry; *The Earl* was officially withdrawn on 31 August 1961, and *Countess* eleven months later on 31 July 1962. Fortunately the preservations were at hand and each has survived on what is now a revitalised heritage railway, one of the 'Great Little Trains of Wales'.

This is the unmistakable vista of Meldon Viaduct just south of Okehampton, with an original Bulleid 'Light Pacific' on an up passenger working, from either Plymouth, Padstow or Bude. This magnificent structure comprising six trusses opened in 1874 and was built on a curve; it is 535 feet long with a maximum height of 120 feet above the valley floor. Able to accommodate a double track, it is of both wrought iron and cast iron and is just one of two surviving wrought iron truss girder railway bridges in the United Kingdom. (The other is the disused Bennerley Viaduct between Awsworth and Ilkeston in the Erewash Valley.) Meldon is supported on tapering trestle sections standing on 24-foot-wide masonry bases. As may be discerned from the photograph, the structure is in an exposed position on the edge of Dartmoor, and that together with the curve necessitated both a speed and weight restriction. The trestles were strengthened in 1938 and again in 1944, both to allow heavier traffic to use the viaduct during the Second World War and to allow for heavier engines. Further strengthening to the trestles was carried out in 1959 and 1960.

Passenger services south of Okehampton were withdrawn in 1968, after which the viaduct reverted to a single track and for a time found a new use as a headshunt for the nearby ballast quarry at Meldon. During this time it was jokingly (but truthfully) referred to as the most expensive (to maintain) headshunt in the world. Then in 1970 a road was built across the viaduct to give lorries access to the Meldon Dam construction site. The bridge was reassessed in 1990 as being too weak to carry trains and the rails were removed. Six years later it was refurbished and reopened as part of The Granite Way, a combined cycle and foot path. Notwithstanding the previous comment as to its condition, there is still the hope that one day the 'missing link' – the lifted track between Okehampton and Bere Alston – may one day be re-established and trains may once again travel through the beautiful scenery at this point.

With the crew keen to be included, 'T9' 4-4-0 No 30289 pauses between shunt moves at Brockenhurst in July 1957. Built at the LSWR's Nine Elms works in February 1900, the members of the 'T9' Class were originally one of the front-line express locomotives of the London & South Western Railway, but gradually slipped away in importance to lesser duties, many working out their final days on the lines west of Exeter. Eastleigh also retained a few for cross-country workings as well as pick-up freight/shunt duties, as seen here. Their ability to run at speed quickly soon earned them the nickname 'Greyhounds', while their abilities on light fast trains saw some members of the class enjoy an Indian summer in the late 1930s and through the Second World War, when they were often used on airways' specials between London Victoria and Poole, frequently working non-stop in each direction. The last of the class was withdrawn in 1963 – No 30289 went towards the end of 1959. One member, No 30120, is preserved as part of the National Collection.

Another locomotive study, and this time it is 'O2' No 30192 shunting at Devonport (Plymouth) on 3 May 1961, with, as recounted later, just three months of active service left. Compared with the pristine condition in which we saw No W35 earlier, this example looks tired and work-stained although there is perhaps some excuse as the image is likely from the late 1950s when the engine was already approaching 70 years of age. In its earliest days the class of sixty, built between 1889 and 1894, had been used on suburban services out of Waterloo – the days before electrification, of course. Their reign, however, was to be short, for the larger 'T1' and 'M7' types began to eclipse the 'O2s' as early as 1897 on the same workings, and the latter were relegated to lighter services over various branch lines, in turn displacing older engines.

Under Southern Railway ownership they were considered as ideal for use on the Isle of Wight and the first two were sent over as early as 1923, the motive power situation on the island lines being identified as critical. The new engines were a success from the start and in total some twenty-three were despatched 'overseas' up to 1949. On the mainland the remainder continued on light duties – light, that is, for the mainland – until the last in service, No 30225, was withdrawn in 1962. No 30192 seen here was a Plymouth Friary engine and was at work until 31 August 1961, after which it was sent to Eastleigh and according to official records scrapped one month later. Notice the long fire iron wedged on top of the tank top.

In this panoramic view of Bangor station on 27 July 1955 there are at least five steam engines and a diesel multiple unit visible. The station is at its infrastructure peak, with four platforms plus a bay. Other facilities included an extensive goods yard, a five-road engine shed with turntable, a three-road goods shed, two signal boxes and an extra footbridge together with a subway. As well as being on the main line to Holyhead, the station was the starting point/destination for several branch services including trains to Bethesda, Carnarvon, Llanberis, Amlwch and Red Wharf Bay. Understandably, as lines closed so the facilities dwindled and by the 1970s the station was reduced to just two operational platforms, although plans are afoot to reinstate at least part of the Amlwch branch as far as Llangefni. In this image one engine, No 40003, may be identified by number, while other types seen are at least one Fairburn 2-6-4T and a brace of 'Black 5s'.

No 40003 itself was one of a class of seventy engines designed by Sir Henry Fowler and introduced in batches between 1930 and 1932. All were built at Derby and while performing sterling service they were later eclipsed by the newer and larger Stanier and Fairburn 2-6-4T classes. In 1948 No 40003 was based at Rugby, but had moved to Bangor in November 1955 – which therefore helps date the image as well. It had moved south to Willesden in August 1957, but was also reported as having been stored at Rugby around this time, so the transfer may well have been more of a paper exercise. Whatever, its final shed was Widnes in August 1960, and from where it was withdrawn in February 1961 and scrapped at the Ince Wagon Works in Wigan. All the class had gone by 1962 with none preserved.

The magnificent arch at the entrance to the locomotive shed at Inverness was recorded on 20 April 1957. Surely no other locomotive depot anywhere in Britain had such a grandiose design. Beyond the arch – which also served as the water tank for the shed – was a semi-circular roundhouse, which closed in 1962 and was demolished the following year. Regretfully the arch was similarly dealt with, the site now being occupied by a supermarket, although the location of the turntable is picked out with stones. (Other views of Inverness will be found later – see the Index).

This is likely one of the earliest colour views in the collection, but regretfully also suffering from some deterioration. The loco is 'L1' 2-6-4T No 67734 in early British Railways livery and attached to former LNER stock in the similarly early 'plum and spilt milk' colours. We are not told the location, but it is likely to be in the vicinity of Liverpool Street. This is the only early view of a Thompson 'L1' to have been found in the collection and illustrates (just) this design of large tank engine, the first having been introduced in May 1945. No 9000, as it was, is also the only one to have been completed under LNER ownership, the remaining twenty-nine from the original order of thirty being completed at Darlington in 1948. A further seventy – it had originally been intended to build eighty – were constructed by the North British Locomotive Co and Messrs Robert Stephenson & Hawthorn between 1948 and 1950.

Despite comprehensive testing of the prototype, a number of weaknesses were discovered in traffic, both mechanical and from an operational perspective. These included axlebox wear and overheating, leakage from the side tanks, and draughty cabs. Various modifications were made, or experimented with, but it is sad to relate that as early as 1955 some of the class were described as being in a 'deplorable' condition – a sad indictment on a modern design. As such, while performing generally good service on suburban and stopping passenger services from a number of depots throughout the Eastern Region, these were the same depots that received some of the first allocations of diesel multiple units, and as a result the 'L1s' were displaced with little further suitable work available for them. The whole one hundred had gone by 1962, with none surviving.

British Railways in Unseen Colour: 1948-1962

A brake van trip is photographed at Rayne on the line between Bishops Stortford and Witham, via Hockerill Halt, Stane Street Halt, Takeley, Easton Lodge, Dunmow, Felstead, Bannister Green Halt, Rayne and Braintree. Passenger services on this route had ceased in March 1952, although goods would continue at the station until December 1964, this trip having been made in July 1959. On many rural routes as passenger numbers declined so freight became the mainstay of lines, with coal invariably the greatest traffic handled. Indeed, up to the 1960s coal was the principal means of heating for most homes, but later it was replaced by a move towards cleaner fuels. This is turn meant the demise of many rural goods yards, their respective coal merchants being forced to move to 'concentration' depots to receive their supplies while at the same time seeing a general downturn in their business. (Remember the days when the coalman was a regular visitor, the sight of such a vehicle now being a rarity.)

On this line, as the various rural goods yards closed there was still some agricultural traffic to Braintree. Following complete closure to all goods at the end of 1971, the future looked bleak, although one final enthusiasts' special was operated from Bishops Stortford as far as Easton Lodge in July of the following year. There had been hope that the route might play a part in carrying additional traffic to Stansted Airport, but proposals came to nothing and in 1974 the track was lifted. A short length of track was reinstated in 2014 and a carriage provided at Rayne station together with a museum and 'The Booking Hall Café' in part of the main buildings. The engine is not identified but may well be a 'J17' 0-6-0.

An LNER 'Y9' (North British Railway 'G') locomotive is seen here as BR No 68095, but the location is not reported. This unusual type of locomotive originated in 1882 when the NBR purchased two in 1882 to an existing standard-design from the builder Neilson & Co. Intended for dock shunting, they proved both suitable and flexible and thirty-eight were then built up to 1899. According to the excellent website on LNER locomotive classes, https://www.lner.info/locos/Y/y9.php, we have at last the origin of the term 'Pug', which has variously applied to a number of small locomotive classes, as well as some interesting information as to their crews. 'Although the term "pug" was used for different engines on different railways (e.g. the Caledonian men called all tank engines "pugs"), the NBR reserved the name "pug" for these engines. Typically, the "Y9s" were crewed by the youngest drivers and firemen. However, senior men would also be posted on the "Y9s" for health reasons, or as a form of demotion for misdemeanours on the main line. Apparently more than one driver known for speeding ended up spending a number of years shunting a "Y9" at Leith Docks!'

Changes over the years included new boilers with repositioned safety valves and an alteration to the coupling rods. Of immediate note are the solid ('dumb') buffers, originally hardwood timber but later given even more strength by being covered over with metal plates; the timber buffer beams were retained. The other item of note is that here was a 'tank engine' fitted with a tender, the result being that they now possessed an increase on the original limited 18cwt of coal that could be carried on the engine alone; even so, this was literally a 'coal cart' as no additional water was carried on this wooden wagon. Attachment between engine and tender was a simple three-link coupling; those engines that were used on the main line were also fitted with safety chains – akin to the fitment seen on carriage stock in the 19th century. Despite their diminutive size and perhaps limited use, thirty-nine entered LNER service, although one was withdrawn in the same year. Twenty-five years later in 1948, thirty-three entered BR service but inroads were made into the type from 1953 onwards and all were out of service by 1962, No w68095 being the last to go on 31 December 1962. Fortunately it was saved and is now in the charge of the Scottish Railway Preservation Society.

'57xx' pannier tank No 4658 is engaged on shunting operations at Doublebois on the Cornish main line west of Liskeard some time in May 1960. Likely this was the daily pick-up goods and the string of empty coal wagons will have been already collected – not necessarily all from here, of course – ready for their long haul back to the collieries at … wherever. Pick-up goods trains like this could run at varying times, and not always according to the timetable. Although an allowance was made for shunting en route, this was by its very nature flexible and would depend on the amount of work required at each location. Should the service get seriously out of sequence, it was not unknown for a longer pause to be made and the train shunted into a loop or 'wrong road', such as here, to allow a scheduled service to pass. Aside from the engine crew, the guard is leaning from his van seemingly in conversation with the fireman (likely to be the fireman as he is on the left of the cab and GWR engines were all right-hand drive). Another member of staff is also to be seen leaning on the gate at the rear of the platform. In the immediate foreground is a GWR/Western Region tubular signal post with a 4-foot metal arm.

It is late spring at Lostwithiel and '14xx' No 1434 pauses in the bay platform between trips on the Fowey branch on 2 May 1954. The fireman (or it may of course be the driver) also takes the opportunity for a break from the heat of the cab and its enjoying a cup of tea. No 1434 is 'auto-fitted', although it is not entirely certain if push-and-pull is the type of working being employed here. Under the canopy the notice board is advertising special offers on tickets to Redruth, St Austell, Truro and Plymouth, although for the present at least there does not appear to be a trong eager to take advantage of the offers. No 4834 was built at Swindon in 1932 as a modern replacement for the '517' Class of the same wheel arrangement. It was renumbered 1434 in November 1946 and retained this number then for the remainder of its life. (The 48xx series as required for some of the engines that were converted to burn oil fuel.) At nationalisation No 1434 is shown as allocated to Machynlleth, but went south in May 1955 to Plymouth Laira, where it remained until withdrawn and condemned seven years later and sold to Messrs Cashmore at Newport for scrap.

Still in the South West, a favourite line among many was the 10¼-mile Princetown branch from Yelverton to the remote Dartmoor settlement. Along the single line there were three intermediate stopping places, at King Tor Halt, Ingra Tor Halt, and Burrator & Sheepstor Halt, the latter the location of the infamous snake notice cautioning walkers of the dangers of adders. Working the line was not easy, as there was a 1 in 40 rising gradient almost all the way from the junction station at Yelverton to Princetown, 1,373 feet above sea level. To work the railway the GWR and Western Region almost exclusively used the '44xx' series 2-6-2 tank engines from their introduction in 1905; these were similar in appearance to the '45xx' type except for having smaller wheels and so being ideal for the steep gradients.

A practice, certainly not unique but definitely unusual, was the use of gravity shunting to run round the branch passenger train at Yelverton. The engine arrived bunker first and, after having disgorged its passengers at Yelverton (disgorged is perhaps the wrong word as it implies that there would be a number – a few is probably more accurate) would then propel its train back towards Princetown for a short distance. Then the Guard would screw down hard the brakes in his van and the engine would be uncoupled and would run back towards the station, being turned into a dead-end siding. Once arrived the points would again be moved and the guard would now release his brake and carefully allow the coaches to roll down into the curved platform, where they would be stopped. The engine would then be released and, after running forward and once more backwards, be reattached to its train. (A similar gravity operation took place when running round at Cowes, and no doubt there were other locations too.) Yelverton itself was on the line from Plymouth to Launceston and boasted the triangular building seen here, which served both the Plymouth-bound platform and that for Princetown seen here.

No 4410 was a Plymouth Laira engine and was withdrawn from service at the end of September 1955, just six months before the Princetown branch was closed and two months after this image was taken on 27 July. In the background a black-liveried – or is it a very dark green? – '14xx' tank engine is on a Launceston train.

'Austerity' 2-8-0 No 400 *Sir Guy Williams* is seen on the Longmoor Military Railway at Whitehill between Longmoor and Borden, seemingly with steam to spare. Built by North British as its No 25205 in 1943, it was immediately loaned to the LNER as 'WD' No 77337 and based at March. Just a few months later it achieved notoriety as the engine at the head of the munitions trains that exploded at Soham; although at the head of the train it was severely damaged. It was returned to North British for repair and by the end of 1944 had arrived in Europe, being used in both France and Holland, returning to Longmoor in 1949. Likely soon after this it was named *Sir Guy Williams* and although at first a conventional coal-burning engine it was latterly converted to burn oil. It operated in this form until 1967 when it was scrapped. (Sir Guy Williams, 1881-1959, served in the Royal Engineers in command of the 8th Brigade, 5th Division Eastern Command.)

Morar station, on the line from Fort William, was the penultimate stopping point before Mallaig, 3 miles further on. Situated on the picturesque West Highland line, the station here was opened as part of the final section of the 67-mile North British Railway route on 1 April 1901 and was photographed 59 years later on May 1960. From Mallaig it is possible to access a ferry service to the Kyle of Lochalsh, Armadale, the Isle of Skye and the Small Isles. Passing through spectacular scenery, including such locations as Rannoch Moor, it is not surprising to report that the Glasgow-Mallaig line has been voted the top railway journey in the world. Corrour station is the summit, at 1,347 feet above sea level, and also has no road access. In the background at Morar is a Camping Coach.

An early type of 'Blue Pullman' perhaps? From the late 1950s onwards a number of former Pullman coaches that had reached the end of their running life were withdrawn and converted to Camping Coaches, based at sites throughout the length and breath of the country. This carried on a tradition that had been started by the pre-nationalisation companies, which had variously referred to the idea as 'Camping', 'Holiday', or 'Caravan' coaches. Prior to the popularity of the continental package holiday, vacations had been very much categorised into one of several types: the holiday camp, bed and breakfast accommodation, or a caravan-type holiday, the latter usually on a fixed site. The railways saw this as an opportunity and were thus keen to enter into what was a lucrative market. It was a solid idea and the popularity of 'Camping Coaches' rose to a peak in 1938/39 before such things were understandably curtailed due to war. After the war, those vehicles that remained were often in poor condition, some having been used as dormitories for workmen and having been left in, shall we say, less than ideal conditions.

This example was at Heacham in East Anglia, the junction for Hunstanton. The Pullman brand was seen as indicating a 'higher class' of accommodation, although it must be remembered there was no heating on a static coach, while comforts were definitely on a 'self-catering' basis. Even basic facilities were lacking – water, for example, was provided and collected in cans or churns. The accommodation was booked on a weekly basis with a requirement that travel to and from the site must be by rail. Clean linen was provided weekly and the vehicle cleaned at the same intervals, between periods of occupancy. Today such an idea may appear basic, but it continued to be a success right though to the mid-1960s, with Pullman cars often used, and sometimes retaining their original Pullman livery, while others, as here, were repainted. Note the small child on the ground close to the working railway, something that would never be allowed today. The 'Camping Coach' concept is still in existence today at a few select locations, although now they are rightly regarded as luxury vehicles operated by private enterprise.

To the enthusiast there was something particular thrilling about visiting an engine shed. To the professional railwayman, especially loco crew or artisans, it was a place of work, invariably poorly equipped, dark, dirty and in general with limited facilities. Indeed, in 1963 the passing of the 'Offices, Shops and Railway Premises Act' – a very early form of 'Health & Safety' at work – specifically excluded steam sheds; to do otherwise would have literally brought the railways to a halt overnight. The excuse was that steam was on the way out and in consequence changes need not be made. A few years before that in March 1958 two engines, Nos 70051 and 42737, are being prepared for work outside Carlisle Kingmoor shed. 'Britannia' No 70051 carried the name *Firth of Forth* and was one of several members of the class that spent much if not all their working lives on the LMR. Built at Crewe in 1954, it had an operational life of just over thirteen years and ended its days as one of more than 200 engines cut up at Shettleston, Glasgow.

No 42737 was un-named, except that the class of 200-plus engines quickly gained the nickname 'Crabs' due to the shape and step of the running plate, visible here. This engine had a somewhat longer working life, also having emerged from Crewe but back in 1927. Just short of forty years later it was withdrawn and disposed of by Messrs Campbell at Airdrie. Kingmoor shed closed on 1 January 1968, eight months before steam finished completely on British Railways. On the same day a new 'Carlisle Kingmoor' depot opened on the opposite side of the main line, but this time servicing diesel locomotives and units. This remained operational until 1987, but then lay derelict until revitalised by the private operator Direct Freight Services. Note on the right-hand side a loco-mounted snowplough stored ready for winter.

Bulleid 'Merchant Navy' No 35027 *Port Line* awaits departure westbound from Brockenhurst in 1957. Completed at Eastleigh at the end of 1948 as one of the final batch of ten members of what would be a thirty-strong class, No 35027 was, like its classmates, rebuilt in the form seen here from 1957 onwards, and for the next decade continued to work on the principal passenger trains on the South Western main lines to Exeter and Weymouth. Upon withdrawal in 1967 No 35027 went first to Barry scrapyard where it rusted for some fifteen years before it was saved and moved initially to the Bluebell Railway for restoration. It subsequently moved again, first to the Swanage Railway, then Southall and later Bury. Restoring, running and also maintaining a steam engine regardless of size or type is both a costly and time-consuming affair and, like every other machine, *Port Line* has had its share of workings, repairs and stoppages, but has also worked special trains on the main line as well as being a popular attraction on various heritage lines.

Working the Princetown branch line was not without incident, especially during poor weather conditions. Indeed, there were several occasions over the years when trains became snowbound for several days. Up to 1930 the railway carried prisoners destined for incarceration at the infamous Dartmoor prison, but this particular traffic ceased in 1930 when the Southern route as far as Tavistock and a road connection was found to be more convenient. Likely prison supplies continued to be handled by rail, while there was also some excursion traffic, and granite was quarried nearby – whether these quarries were to do with the prison is not reported. In this photograph we are looking towards the buffers at the terminus at Princetown. The engine has already run round its train and will shortly set off again for Yelverton; trains were sometimes solely passenger, but operation as mixed trains – passenger and goods – was commonplace, with goods wagons and a brake van attached at the rear. On the extreme right is the small engine shed with the other accoutrements of a typical terminus also present: goods shed, assorted rail wagons, spare passenger coach, supplies for the permanent way gang, etc. Note too the granite-built signal box, which appears to be in the course of being painted. It was often joked that seeing the painters arrive meant that closure would soon follow, and indeed this was to be the case as the Princetown branch railway closed to all traffic in 1956.

This is Saltash again, this time with '64xx' No 6419 on a local working This engine was a long-term resident of Plymouth Laira, one of five members of the class based there in 1947. There is no date for the image, but the tank side has the later BR emblem and there is a suggestion of green under a certain amount of grime – so it is after 1957. The '64xx' type locos were 'auto-fitted', and those in the area were used on both 'auto' (push-pull) and local workings until either their duties were taken over by diesel multiple units or the lines they served were closed. This resulted in withdrawals and transfers, No 6419 ending its days at Yeovil Town at the end of 1964. Here at Saltash the crew have just replenished the water tanks – note the brazier stored ready for winter use. Located in a necessarily cramped position, there was a small goods yard at the western end of the site. The speed of trains through the platforms was also always slow, as at the eastern end the line went onto the Saltash bridge where there was a 15mph speed restriction in both directions. In addition, the single line over the bridge was for many years worked by token, and it was necessary to collect the token at one end and set it down at the other.

The station buildings of the Corris Railway at Machynlleth in mid-Wales were hard by the standard-gauge station of the same name. This photograph was taken on 23 June 1956 at a time when the 2ft 3in-gauge railway had already been closed for some eight years. The line had started life back in the 1850s as a horse- and gravity-worked tramway carrying mined slate from quarries at Corris Uchaf and Aberllefenni in southern Merionethshire to the nearest navigable point on the Afon Dyfi (River Dovey), where it was loaded into ships and carried to its diverse destinations. Soon after, in the 1860s, the line ceased to use shipping and instead slate was brought to the standard-gauge railway at Machynlleth, where it was necessary to tranship it into standard-gauge wagons for distribution. Despite this apparent disadvantage, it must be recalled that this was a time when labour was cheap and plentiful, and Welsh slate enjoyed an enviable reputation as a building product far beyond these shores.

A semi-official passenger service, using adapted wagons, flourished on the Corris in the early 1870s. A more official service using steam power and with proper passenger-carrying vehicles was provided on a regular basis from about 1883, and continued until around 1930. By this time the Great Western Railway had purchased the undertaking, although the slate traffic had reduced considerably. Even so, it continued to be used for goods until 1948 when flood water from Afon Dyfi undermined an embankment on the south side of Dyfi bridge, although the track itself was never actually breached. Fortunately the two Corris locomotives had already been brought to safety at Machynlleth, together with several items of goods stock, and there they remained stored until 1951.

Meanwhile track-lifting was taking place, the Aberllefenni to Corris section being lifted in November 1948, and 10 tons of the rail was purchased by Henry Haydn Jones for use on his Talyllyn Railway, which shared the same gauge. By the end of 1950 track-lifting had reached Machynlleth station. Fortunately the same benefactor came to the rescue of the locomotives and stock, and they are now to be found on the Talyllyn Railway. There matters might have rested except that in 1966 a group of enthusiasts set about restoring the name and the railway, and a short length of demonstration track was laid at Corris in 1971. Today the route extends from Corris as far as Maespoeth, with the avowed aim of eventually returning to Machynlleth. Both the former Corris engines have also made visits to the line on occasions. In the background of this picture is a standard-gauge cattle wagon.

Here is another 'WD' engine, this one in BR service as No 90626. A member of a particularly numerous class, 935 were built to the design of R. A. Riddles between 1943 and 1945. The majority, 545, were built by the North British Locomotive Company at either its works at Hyde Park or Queen's Park in Glasgow, the balance of 390 coming from the Vulcan Foundry at Newton-le-Willows. All but three of the total saw service with the British Army in mainland Europe following D-Day. The design was based on the standard Second World War freight locomotive, the LMS 8F 2-8-0, but with efforts made to reduce manufacturing costs; consequently the firebox was round instead of the Belpaire shape, the boiler parallel instead of being tapered, and the inner firebox made of steel instead of copper. As peace returned so the War Department began to dispose of the engines. There were 930 engines available – three had been scrapped/written off in consequence of accidents in Germany, and two were retained by the WD (we have already seen one of them, *Sir Guy Williams*). One engine went to America, twelve to Hong Kong, and 184 to the Netherlands Railways (two of these subsequently ended up in Sweden).

That left 733 in the UK, 200 of which were purchased by the LNER, which classified them as Class 'O7' and numbered them 3000-3199. Timescales now become slightly confusing, but what is certain is that in 1948 the remaining 533 were purchased by the British Transport Commission, which, together with those from the LNER, numbered them 90000 to 90732. The final locomotive was the only one to carry a name, *Vulcan*. All but two of this large class were still in service in the summer of 1962, but their numbers depleted rapidly and all had gone before the official end of steam in the summer of 1968. Folklore has it that the type were not always popular with crews, rough riding being the principal complaint, even at the slow speeds that goods engines worked. Likely this was exacerbated as the engines became worn out prior to overhaul. Ironically, despite being a numerically large class, none of those working on BR escaped the scrap merchant, the preservationists naturally concentrating on the more popular engine types. This left a gap in the ranks of preserved locos, but fortunately a member of the type was repatriated from Sweden to the Keighley & Worth Valley Railway and has taken the number 90733.

The example seen here appears in reasonable external condition and is pictured with a typical load for the class, namely freight, passing Cheddington on the former LNWR main line between Leighton Buzzard and Berkhamsted.

British Railways in Unseen Colour: 1948-1962

These two views of London Transport 'ESL' (Electric Sleet Locomotives) and brush gear were taken at the depot at Neasden. They were a good example of 'make do and mend', as each locomotive was built at the LT Acton Works by combining the parts from two former Central Line driving motor cars dating from 1903. As might be expected, these machines were used to deliver de-icing facilities to the conductor rails on the open-air sections of the 'Underground'. A total of eighteen were constructed in 1939/40 with the slightly unusual design of four bogies per vehicle; the two central bogies were the 'works' and contained brushes, ice-crushers and spraying gear. Anti-freeze was carried in two 75-gallon tanks. The locomotives were operative until the early 1980s, when de-icing gear was fitted to conventional passenger stock. One of the type, No ESL107, is preserved by London Transport and is restored to what was the original maroon-yellow-black livery. Seen here are four of the locos, although only two, Nos ESL104 and WSL110, can be positively identified.

Still with London Transport, this is 'F' Class 0-6-2T No L50 in resplendent red livery at Neasden on 1 June 1957, yet nearing the end of its life. This particular machine was one of a total of 116 steam engines operated by the Metropolitan Railway over the years, and one of four built by the Yorkshire Engine Company in 1901 with 5-foot driving wheels. Given the numbers 90-93 by the Metropolitan, they later became Nos L49-52 when that company was absorbed into the London Passenger Transport Board in 1933. We tend to forget that some of what became London Transport lines also once carried freight, and this design was intended for freight traffic on the Metropolitan extension and as such were not provided with steam heating equipment. At some stage No L50 has also been equipped for Westinghouse air-braking, as can be seen from the 'donkey pump' and the air reservoir on top of the side tank. The design was basically similar to the earlier 'E' Class, except that the latter had a 0-4-4T wheel arrangement with 5ft 6in driving wheels and was therefore more suitable for passenger working. The 'F' Class also had a greater coal and water capacity than its passenger counterpart and was well capable of working the heaviest goods trains on the line. All four were withdrawn for scrap between 1957 and 1962, with none preserved.

No difficulties here in identification: this is Adams 'Radial' tank No 30583 in the bay platform at Axminster in the process of running around its branch train for Lyme Regis. This was a definite veteran at this time, the design dating back to 1882 and one of a class of seventy-one engines. three of which survived into British Railways days. Originally built for suburban traffic and working alongside the 'O2' type seen earlier, the arrival of the 'M7' design displaced both the 'O2s' and what was officially the '415' Class. Unlike the 'O2' design, though, little suitable work was found for the type and most had gone by the time of the Grouping in 1923; the last two in service, latterly working trains on the Lyme Regis branch, were withdrawn in 1929. Unfortunately the replacements sent to work the branch, LBSCR 'D1' tank engines, were quickly found unsuitable and an order was given for the two retired 4-4-2Ts to be reinstated. They were consequently taken off the scrapping list and overhauled at Eastleigh for further duty.

The Lyme Regis branch, on the border of Devon and Dorset, commenced with a junction at the Devon town of Axminster – famed for its carpets – and wound its way south-east to the Dorset terminus at Lyme Regis, with various weight and speed restrictions and sharp curves on the way. Operating the line had been a trial for many years, and while loads were not necessarily a problem, flange wear with other types of engine was. The Adams 'Radial', however, was found to be less affected, due to the radial action of its trailing truck, hence the need to retain the two engines. In 1946 a third was sourced from the East Kent Railway, having been sold out of service in 1917 and eventually finding its way to that outpost of the Colonel Stephens empire. As BR Nos 30583-5, they were all based at Exmouth Junction and continued to work the line until 1961 when age dictated their withdrawal. Fortunately No 30583 was saved by the Bluebell Railway. Thereafter BR had no option but to affect improvements, and the last years of steam on the branch saw Ivatt Class 2 engines operating services. These were then replaced by diesel railcars until the branch was closed under the Beeching cuts in 1965.

ABOVE LNER outer-suburban. 'N7' 0-6-2T No 69691, on an Upminster to Grays train, passes the signal box at West Thurrock Junction on 23 March 1957. To the left the track heads towards Purfleet and Barking. Notice the flat-bottom and bullhead rails on the two lines. The 'N7' design dated back to 1915, with the first of the class introduced on the Great Eastern Railway to the designs of Alfred John Hill. Unusually the class had inside Walschaerts valve gear and, as was GER practice for suburban passenger trains, was also fitted with Westinghouse air brakes. The type would eventually number 134 engines, introduced between 1915 and 1928, and encompassed several variations. No 69691, previously LNER No 2651 then No 9691, was supplied by William Beardmore & Co in 1927, and was designated 'N7/2', having a Belpaire firebox and long-travel valves. The class was intact at the start of 1957, but the first withdrawal, of No 69689, occurred in that year. After that a number were taken out of service in consecutive years, No 69691 being one of forty-five that ceased work in 1960. The final nine were taken out of service in 1962. One has been preserved and is on static display at the East Anglian Railway Museum at Chappel & Wakes Colne pending overhaul. The class led an uneventful but useful life, marred perhaps by one incident that, although serious at the time, is not perhaps without a touch of humour. It occurred on 24 May 1954 when sister engine No 69638 ran into the turntable pit at Hatfield, Hertfordshire – following the removal of the actual turntable.

RIGHT The London & North Western Railway was an early player in the electrification stakes, the first of its electric trains arriving in 1914. Operating on a fourth-rail 630V system, the sphere of operation was from London Broad Street, where this view was taken, to Richmond, and Euston to Watford, together with the branch lines to Croxley Green and Rickmansworth. There were also links to the District Railway at Earls Court and Richmond. Formed into three-car sets, there was mixed seating for thirty-three 1st and 130 3rd Class passengers, the latter a mixture of longitudinal and facing pairs of seats. Seen here is car No 28290, one of a number of vehicles known as Oerlikon stock due to the type of electrical equipment fitted. In LMS days this car was, as seen here, in crimson livery and was classified DMBT (Driving Motor Brake Third). During BR days the stock was repainted in Southern-type green, then the standard for EMU stock. No date is given for the image, but we may take it as being one of Roy's earlier colour photographs.

British Railways in Unseen Colour: 1948-1962

The mainstay of the fast passenger fleet of the Great Western Railway and Western Region of British Railways for almost forty years were the 171 members of the 'Castle' Class. The actual number built is used advisedly as it must be pointed out that the first had been withdrawn before the last was built, so, even allowing for those temporarily out of use 'in works', the full number were never actually on the books at the same time. The figure quoted also included several that had been reconstructed from engines of the 'Star' Class, the first of the 'Castle' Class design being built in 1923 and the last leaving service in 1965. They were to be found dispersed throughout the GWR/WR system and were never fully displaced by the advent of the BR Standard designs in the early days of BR. They were built in batches from 1923 onwards, the earliest engines having bogie brakes – later removed – and small 3,500-gallon tenders. As time passed so further modifications were made, including larger tenders and a higher degree of superheat, while towards the end engines were modified with a double chimney, although aesthetically still keeping the copper top and capuchon.

No 5024 *Carew Castle* is seen here 'on shed' at Newton Abbot in April 1956, facing in the direction of Plymouth. No lamp headcode has been added so we cannot confirm what its next duty might be. This was the home shed for this engine, as shown by the 83A shedplate, and from here it might work west to Plymouth and on into Cornwall – perhaps double-heading a westbound train over the South Devon banks – north towards Bristol and beyond, or east to London. No 5024 appears serviced, with a generous loading of coal and the front coupling stowed correctly, thus possibly ready for work; a light haze of smoke emanates from the chimney. The paintwork has probably been wiped over, although it has perhaps not received as much attention from the cleaners as might be wished. Notice also how the boiler handrail has taken a bash at some stage. In the background other engines are being prepared, while a red auto-coach is on the dead-end siding alongside the tender.

No 6873 *Caradoc Grange* heads east past Laira Junction, Plymouth, with a stopping passenger train bound perhaps for Exeter on 15 July 1957. The signal box of the same name is on the left, and not only controlled operations on the main line but also the route to Mount Gould Junction, referred to earlier. Laira steam shed is in the left background. Two things are of particular interest. In the extreme bottom left-hand corner is a small section of the 4-foot-gauge Lee Moor Tramway, identified by the timber infill between the rails; this was a horse-drawn system that crossed the main railway at this point by means of a level crossing. On the right the carriage sidings contain a wonderful array of vehicles of Great Western design, including 'Toplight' and, ever more especially, auto-coaches, both close by and in the distance. Notice too the ladder crossing consisting of a number of double-slip points affording access to all the sidings. In the distance on the extreme right it is just possible to make out the cylindrical shape of a 'Cordon'; these were gas tank wagons whose contents were used to charge the tanks of gas-lit coaches as required. Some of the auto-coaches certainly fit into this category, hence the presence of the wagon. When supplies had been exhausted a replacement was sent from the gasworks at Swindon. Just in front of the signal box, the smoke-blackened ringed signal arms control access into the goods loops.

Dignity and impudence at Neasden shed, 34E. We have three engines in view, and on the extreme left that essential component of all large steam sheds, the breakdown crane. No 67416 was a J. G. Robinson design of 4-4-2T originally built for the Great Central Railway but absorbed into the LNER in 1923, where it was given the class designation 'C13'. (Post-1946 the LNER resolved to sort out a somewhat chaotic numbering sequence that existed with its steam fleet and tackled this Herculean task by designating a class letter to each wheel arrangement. Thus 'A' was for a 4-6-2, 'B' a 4-6-0, 'C' a 4-4-2, etc. The numbering that followed relating to the individual grounds of engines.) Introduced from 1903, some, supposedly including No 67416, were push-pull-fitted, although this equipment has probably been removed as there does not appear to be any trace of it at the front.

No 42249 is easier to define, being a modern 2-6-4T engine, similar in many ways to the later BR '80000' series. This particular example was to a Fairburn design that first took to the rails in 1945 and was a good general-purpose machine. Notice the oval buffers, fitted when there was a risk of buffer-lock, especially when propelling on sharp curves. Of note on both engines are the guard irons coming down ahead of the front wheels and intended to cast aside any small items of debris on the rails that might otherwise be at risk of causing a derailment.

Finally on the right we have a modern BR Standard Class 4 tender engine, No 76040. Accessible and generally popular with the crews, except that is where company favouritism perhaps influenced a more subjective assessment, this type was designed at Doncaster with examples seen on most of the regions of BR. However, on film is the only place where these three engines still exist, as all were eventually destined for scrap.

First-generation Metropolitan-Cammell twin-unit DMU calls at Mundesley-on-Sea station, Norfolk, on 21 March 1960. At this time the station became in effect a terminus as the remainder of the line north to Cromer closed. Previous to this it had been part of the Norfolk & Suffolk Joint Railway running from Antingham Road Junction beyond North Walsham to join the Midland & Great Northern line at Runton West Junction. Opened in 1898 between North Walsham and Mundesley, then on to Cromer in 1906, the facilities here included three wide platforms, 600 feet long – the third is out of sight to the left – together with substantial buildings and a yard for anticipated holiday traffic, which might explain the presence of an LNER-liveried green and white coach on the extreme right. Indeed, up to five LNER 'Caravan Coaches' might be stabled here for the season and were booked as required. Unfortunately diesel sets failed to revive the traffic and the remaining passenger services were withdrawn on 5 October 1964, with freight succumbing a year later. Nothing remains of the location today, which has been redeveloped as a housing estate

Double-heading on the Somerset & Dorset line on 5 September 1959 sees an LMS 2P and BR 'Standard 5' No 73087 in charge of a train of Midland stock, likely an excursion, recorded near Midford. The 71-mile S&D route between Bath and Bournemouth was aptly described by the late Ivo Peters as 'An English Cross Country Railway' – totally accurate, but perhaps not in so few words conjuring up all the charm of this much-lamented route. Conceived back in the 19th century as an amalgam of two companies, it variously had independence and was then passed into the joint hands of the Midland and London & South Western companies, later continuing that joint arrangement with the LMS and Southern. It can often be the case that such joint arrangements are difficult to administer, but the S&D flourished and found a use both as a local route and also the home of the iconic 'Pines Express'. Summer weekends would also see a veritable procession of trains from the North and the Midlands taking the line for the final part of the journey to the coast, a similar movement occurring later in the day for the return workings.

Unfortunately, though, the route also had its failings: a reversal at Bath Green Park was required, trains were subjected to varying lengths of single line, and most of all the severe gradients that necessitated double-heading for the heaviest trains, as indeed is seen here. Together with a transfer of control to the Western Region in the late 1950s, which was widely known to have no love for the railway, all would combine to see timetables altered, through traffic rerouted and a railway left that was expensive to operate but which could not hope to survive on local traffic alone. To the railwaymen working the line it was a slow decline, accelerated from the summer of 1962 when the 'Pines Express' was rerouted away. Somehow, though, the line lingered on until March 1966, the final three months seeing an emergency timetable introduced as the replacement bus services were not ready. The renowned and much-loved poet John Betjeman waxed lyrical about the railway, and almost in the same vein we can understand the sadness when the local hostelry at Evercreech Junction changed it name at the time of closure to 'The Silent Whistle'.

At Devonport Junction a pair of North British diesel-hydraulics in the D63xx series make their way on the WR line eastwards towards Plymouth. Nearest the camera is the Southern line from Okehampton, hence the difference in signals: lower-quadrant on the WR route and upper-quadrant for the Southern. Already, though, change is in the air, as witness the MAS (multiple aspect signalling) post, for the present out of use with its 'X' box covering the signal head.

Known as 'Baby Warships', the D63xx Type 2 (later Class 22) locomotives were a class of fifty-eight engines that entered service from the North British Locomotive Company in 1959-62. Initially plagued with reliability issues, these were later overcome although by that time their intended use on main-line workings had already been taken over by the 'Hymek' and 'Warship' classes. In consequence they found work on lighter duties, with many based in the West. Unfortunately three situations out of their control were ranged against them: the closure of lines over which they had operated, NBL ceasing to trade and a consequent lack of spares, and the general preference for diesel-electric rather than hydraulic transmission that was beginning to creep across BR. Consequently engines were being withdrawn for spares and the class was extinct at the end of 1971. One engine was purchased privately for preservation but was cut up at Swindon before it could be taken away.

Midland Railway Johnson 3F 0-6-0 No 47236 poses at Burton in September 1957. For many years the standard MR and LMS small shunting engine, this particular example had been at Burton since August 1956, having previously been at Sheffield Grimesthorpe and latterly Derby, then Carlisle. Built for the Midland by Vulcan Foundry, sixty engines of the type were introduced from 1899 onwards and lasted into British Railways days. A development soon into LMS days in 1924 was a further 400-plus engines to the same basic design, the whole subsequently given the nickname 'Jinties'. Seen here with the first BR crest, an oil can on the front framing, and working on shunting duty '104', No 47236 has a few years of useful life remaining before withdrawal in the summer of 1964. Notice the two couplings hanging on the draw hook.

The story – nay, legend – of *City of Truro* has been told many times previously so only need be reported in précis form here. Suffice to say, twenty engines of the class were built at Swindon between 1902 and 1909, while ten other earlier engines of the 4-4-0 type were modified to the same style in the same period. Originally numbered in the 37xx series, the locos quickly became renowned for their speed and haulage, thanks to large-diameter driving wheels, and were entrusted with the fastest and heaviest trains. Their reign, though, was to be brief as loads became ever heavier, but before that one member of the class, No 3440 *City of Truro* achieved notoriety with a claimed 102.3mph while descending Wellington bank in Somerset on 9 May 1904, the first time a speed in excess of 100mph had been claimed for a steam locomotive. Almost since that very date debate has raged over the accuracy of the measurement. Whatever, *City of Truro* was travelling fast, very fast indeed, but recent evidence tends to point to a maximum of perhaps just over 100 rather than the 102.3 claimed.

It matters not, as its place in history was assured and upon withdrawal in 1931 it was 'stuffed and mounted' in the original York Railway Museum. There it remained until the Western Region decided to resurrect it, and it was returned to Swindon for overhaul and use both in everyday service and on special trains. So far as the former were concerned, this meant that it was based at Didcot and worked a daily out-and-back diagram on the Didcot, Newbury & Southampton line. Curiously, the up or return journey was scheduled to call at Eastleigh shortly after the day shift had completed its shift at the nearby works and would thus carry a number of workers north back to Winchester. Coincidence, perhaps, or the impish behaviour of the Western Region in showing 'that Southern lot' what the best of Swindon could do! As mentioned, the engine also operated a number of special trains, an early one shown here on 16 June 1957 with a Stephenson Locomotive Society (Midland area) tour from Wolverhampton to Swindon Works and return. The engine is seen in the works yard attached to what was a not inconsiderable train of Mk 1 coaches. It was also reported that on the return run 85mph was achieved at Leamington Spa. *City of Truro* survives today as part of the National Collection, and since the demise of main-line steam has seen service on a number of preserved lines over the decades.

A slight touch of camera shake on this one is not helped by the speed of the train versus the available speed of the film. There is some positive identification, though, for this is No 70005 *John Milton* at Audley End on the former Great Eastern line with a London-bound express working in July 1958. A purely personal opinion here, but the 'crimson and cream' ('blood and custard' and similar variants) livery for the coaching stock went so well with a green engine. To be fair, the engine itself is a bit work-grimed, but the effect is still there. There are two main running lines here as well as up and down loops, that nearest the camera on concrete sleepers with bullhead track, the same type as on the far side. The main running lines have the heavier flat-bottom rail, but still in short 60-foot lengths. Another lost aspect of the steam age is the telegraph pole, more accurately part of the pole route by means of which signal boxes and the railway telephone network could communicate. Unfortunately, being exposed this was prone to weather damage and also the behaviour of certain members of society who would steal the copper cable for scrap.

Three proud men: on the left is Driver Strains, centre Inspector Wally Mason, and Fireman Smith, believed to have been photographed on 14 May 1959, the day when Roy had a footplate trip to Norwich. No 70000 *Britannia* was the very first of the BR Standard designs and was built at Crewe. It entered service at Stratford on 5 January 1951 and remained there for eight years until moving to Norwich Thorpe on 31 January 1959 as dieselisation and electrification progressed on the GE lines. The latter prompted a move to Willesden on 30 March 1963, followed by Crewe North on 25 March of the same year, and Crewe South just four days later. Its final allocation was at Newton Heath (Manchester) from 5 March 1966, from where it was withdrawn on 28 May 1966 after a life of just 15 years, 4 months and 23 days. Originally intended for preservation as part of the National Collection, No 70000 was eventually passed over for sister engine No 70013, the stated reason being that No 70013 was more representative of the class compared with the prototype. It was, however, reported in the contemporary railway press that the change had been due to No 70000 being badly vandalised following withdrawal. Whatever the truth, it was fortunate that the Britannia Locomotive Company Ltd was set up and saved this valuable asset. It has since passed through various hands, including several major overhauls and repairs, and is currently in the hands of the Royal Scot Locomotive & General Trust.

In the image the detail of the cab area shows up well. Note especially the rubber bellows between the cab and tender intended to reduce draughts to which the Standard designs generally were prone when running fast. The tender framing is also at a lower level than the main cab, and an accumulation of coal and other deposits may be seen on it. She would no doubt shine up well given some elbow grease and a few oily rags…

Here is another engine on the scrap line at Stratford in April 1955 – we saw No 62788 earlier. 'D16/3' 4-4-0 No 62601 was a member of the 'Claud Hamilton' Class, a design dating back to 1900. Built to the design of William Holden in 1911, it was subsequently modified with a larger boiler and 8-inch piston valves in 1929, which were then increased further to 9½ inches in 1944. The next change came in 1946, although this was purely cosmetic, when the number was changed from LNER 7660 to 2601, finally becoming No 62601 in 1950. At this stage it was allocated to Cambridge, and although not withdrawn until 1 January 1957 it is unlikely that it worked further after this photograph was taken.

Happier times for an engine of the same wheel arrangement: here is beautifully clean 'D1' No 31489 at Ramsgate on 14 September 1960. The number of 4-4-0s existing on the Southern Region by this time was diminishing rapidly – even the superb 'Schools' Class was culled by the stroke of a pen two years later. No 31489, though, has survived to receive a repaint and the later BR crest, and at the time was allocated to Bricklayers Arms; it is likely then that the engine has worked down to Kent and is being made ready for the return. A surfeit of steam following the inauguration of the Kent Coast electrification scheme would see several of the former SECR 4-4-0s transferred to the western section of the SR at Nine Elms, although there was little work for them there either. Despite its pristine appearance, No 31489 would be withdrawn in November 1961 and was dismantled soon after. None of the type survived.

The Somerset & Dorset again, this time featuring one of the unique 2-8-0s designed specifically for the route, the first of the class being introduced in 1914. No 53805 is seen here on a typical duty for the class, heavy freight, which these powerful engines would haul unaided over the fearsome gradients of the line north of Evercreech. The engine appears to be about to start south from the S&D station at Shepton Mallet (there was also a Shepton Mallet station on the Great Western line from Witham to Yatton, but with no physical connection between the two), although for the moment at least the fireman appears occupied atop the tender. On busy summer Saturdays these goods engines would sometimes be pressed into passenger service, although according to *Somerset & Dorset Engineman* Peter Smith, they were not totally happy on these duties and tended to knock and squeal, often due to limited lubrication. Winter saw them revert solely to goods workings as they were not fitted for steam heating. No 53805 was photographed working the 12.35pm Bath to Evercreech service on 26 September 1959, and would survive until 1961. Two other members of the nine-strong class have been preserved.

OPPOSITE TOP The second member of the BR Standard 'Clan' Class, No 72001 *Clan Cameron*, is recorded at an unreported location. Ten members of the type were introduced from Derby in 1951/52, with another fifteen planned, although due to acute steel shortages the order was continually postponed until it was subsequently cancelled consequent upon the publication of the BR Modernisation Plan, which foretold the end of steam. It might well be said that the raison d'être for the type could be traced back to the 1948 Interchange Trials and the performance of the Bulleid 'Light Pacific' type on the former Highland Railway line to Inverness. Here the interloper performed remarkable feats of haulage, which led BR to consider an equivalent two-cylinder engine for this work. As a result all ten 'Clans' were allocated to Scotland, where with familiar crews they gradually gained a good reputation. Unfortunately in the hands of strangers their reception was more mixed, men used to the similar-looking but larger 'Britannia' type finding them shy for steam, perhaps not surprising as they tended to be allocated the same type of work.

Of the intended further fifteen, five would have been allocated to the Southern Region, a slightly strange idea, especially since the SR already had 140 'Pacific'-type engines, far more than the any of the other regions (the Western Region, of course, had none that were 'home-grown'). These five would have worked the heavily graded Somerset & Dorset line and it would certainly have been interesting to see how they performed, considering that the Bulleid 'Light Pacifics' were not exactly well thought of on that line. The ten that were built spent most of their lives in Scotland and the north, but on the very odd occasion one was seen in Wales, Bristol or London, but never further south. A member of the class was even tested on the Eastern Region working out of Stratford for a month in 1958. The first five were withdrawn en masse from Glasgow Polmadie at the end of 1962 and initially stored. They eventually moved to Darlington for scrap in 1964. (Through services over the Somerset & Dorset had ceased in 1962, so there was little point in transferring the stored engines south at that time.) The final five were set aside between April 1965 and May 1966, all being scrapped and none preserved. But, like the phoenix, a new member, No 72010 to be named *Hengist*, is slowly but surely being built from nothing and will one day be seen running as an example of the design.

ABOVE Seemingly fresh from the paint shop – so no wonder the driver is smiling! – LNER 'B17' No 61661 is depicted at Marylebone on 6 April 1949. The engine is in LNER Apple Green but with its BR number applied, and may well have been there for inspection or a special duty. All of the 'B2'/'B17' Class – of which there were variants within the class – were named, many after the football clubs at locations served by the LNER, although the inclusion of Liverpool and Everton in the list was perhaps stretching it slightly. Other names included several 'Halls' and 'Castles', almost as if to prove that the Great Western did not have a monopoly on such names. It is slightly unfortunate that Roy Vincent did not appear to have recorded on film the various short-lived and experimental liveries that appeared around this time. No 61661 was built at Darlington in 1936 and had a life of 23 years, being withdrawn for scrap in July 1959.

OPPOSITE BOTTOM No W34W, one of the GWR-built 'razor-edge' diesel railcars – this one constructed specially for parcels use – is seen at Westbourne Park on the outskirts of Paddington travelling towards the terminus; the edge of the platform at the LT Royal Oak station is just visible on the extreme left. The GWR was a pioneer in the use of diesel railcars, the first single car being introduced in 1933 and intended as a replacement for steam on a fast service between Cardiff and Birmingham. Ironically it was a victim of its own success and steam-hauled trains had to be substituted later as the diesel was proving too popular! At total of thirty-six would eventually be built, those up to No 17 operating solely as single cars, while No 18 was a prototype for branch-line use and was equipped with buffers and drawgear; it would spent its first years of service operating the 12-mile Lambourn branch from Newbury, and was often seen with a trailer coach and horsebox in tow. Later two-car units were introduced, while by modification it was also possible to add an intermediate centre coach.

Seen here is one of the two parcels cars from the build – the other was No 17 of the earlier streamlined type – and they were mainly used in either the London or Gloucester areas. As may be seen from the buffing gear, No W34W was capable of hauling a coach or vans, although haulage power was necessarily limited. Based mainly at Southall, it remained on these duties until 1960 when it was replaced by 'first-generation' parcels cars, again operating a similar service. Three of the GWR railcars have been saved, although neither of the parcels type; No 4 from the original batch is part of the National Collection, while the Kent & East Sussex Railway and the Great Western Society each have a passenger-carrying 'razor-edge' vehicle.

This delightful study of 'Dukedog' No 9018 was taken at Machynlleth on 23 June 1950. The 'Dukedog' Class of 4-4-0 was an amalgam of the frames from a 'Bulldog' Class engine together with the boiler, cylinders, motion and cab from a 'Duke' Class. The origins of the type – the last outside-frame design to be 'built' in the UK – were back in 1929 when, with the thought of improving motive power on the now absorbed Cambrian lines, Swindon combined the two parts referred to for work specifically on that route. Why this combination was chosen is simply because the frames of many of the 'Duke' Class were by now in good condition, yet a small(ish) 4-4-0 was still required for a system where weight restrictions, steep gradients and sharp curves precluded the use of larger engines at that time. No 3265 *Tre Pol and Pen* was the first conversion and was followed by a further twenty-nine 'new' engines – conversions or rebuilds might be more accurate – from 1936 onwards. A further eleven pairs were due to be converted, but the Second World War curtailed the work and several of both the 'Duke' and 'Bulldog' Class engines ended their days unconverted.

As is fairly well known, the conversions were intended to be given the names of Earls, and some were indeed so graced, but legend has it that the individuals whose names were applied objected to them appearing on such a small engine, and they were hurriedly fitted to 'Castle' Class engines instead; from that time, the 32xx series ran unnamed. Renumbering of the 'Dukedogs' together with the remaining 'Dukes' took place in 1946, and the first two digits from each 32xx number were replaced by 90; the 32xx series of numbers was being allocated to new-build Collett 0-6-0 tender engines of the '2251' type. Members of the class were in service until the late 1950s, mostly on the Cambrian but some elsewhere, until strengthening of the infrastructure on that system allowed larger and more modern engines to traverse it. Withdrawal occurred during the period 1948-60.

At the time of the photograph No 9018 was allocated to the Cambrian, but in late 1952 it migrated to Oxford, although its stay there was brief as it was back at Machynlleth again in July 1953. It remained on the Cambrian system until withdrawn in July 1959. One member of the class, No 3217, to quote its original number, and carrying the originally intended name *Earl Berkeley*, is preserved and is based on the Bluebell Railway.

LEFT A unique slide from the collection is this view of the signal box at Edenbridge, taken on 4 June 1955. The term 'unique' is used as it is most definitely a 'stand-alone' view with no others seemingly having been taken in the vicinity, or indeed specifically of signal boxes. There were two stations at Edenbridge, one on the west-to-east SER route between Redhill and Ashford, and the other on the north-to-south LBSCR line from Groombridge Junction towards Uckfield, among other places. Edenbridge Town, on the latter line, dates from 1888 with the signal box dating from the same time. Inside was a 24-lever Saxby & Farmer frame with the levers at 5-inch centres. The name change with the suffix 'Town' took place in 1896, but other than a change to tappet locking in 1908, little alteration was made during its life. The box closed when mechanical signalling was declared redundant in the area from 12 May 1976. Signalmen could be as proud of their signal boxes as some footplatemen were of their engines, the interior kept spotless, the floor polished, levers burnished and instrument brasses shining. Naturally Southern green is also the dominant colour.

BELOW RIGHT Things go wrong sometimes, as at Hither Green on 20 February 1960. In the early morning of 20 February No 34084 *253 Squadron* ran out of rails after failing to stop at the end of the up goods loop. The engine had been in charge of a Dover Marine to Bricklayer's Arms van train. A short run-off siding at the end of the loop had been provided to prevent a run-past such as this from fouling the main line, although the margin for safety was short and certainly insufficient to prevent No 34084 from continuing on as it ran out of track and fell over to one side. Fortunately none of the running lines were blocked but there was considerable disruption to services, a number of signalling cables having been severed. Temporary signalling repairs were made as a matter of priority, with services able to pass as normal the following day. Rerailing was effected by tying rails to the wheels of No 34084 so that once is was upright it could be pulled away relatively easily. To achieve this a path was cleared underneath, and it was also necessary to provide support to prevent further movement. The vital part was that the wheels and tyres needed to be exposed, at which stage lengths of bullhead rail were tied on to the edge of the tyres, but with the rail turned through 90° compared with how it would be laid for normal running; the engine's tyres were thus in a groove. With the 86-ton engine rotated through 90° it was then firmly secured to prevent further movement and was then initially winched and later pulled back on to the rails proper.

It had been intended to recover the engine on 24 February, but fate lent a hand with the derailment of a diesel shunter nearby. The breakdown crew therefore had to attend to this instead, although the drawbar between the engine and tender of No 34084 and the tender itself were successfully removed the same day. A second, this time successful, attempt was made on Sunday 28 February, eight days after the incident. Two cranes, from Stewarts Lane and Bricklayers Arms, were used and these, aided by jacks, pulled the engine to the vertical and by 3.30pm it was restored to the rails. Damage was more superficial than serious and it was towed to Eastleigh and repaired there in April of the same year.

No 34084 had an interesting career as even years earlier it had been one of a pair of 'Battle of Britain' engines involved in a 'coming together' outside Victoria. It also had the melancholy duty of pulling the last steam-hauled weekday up 'Atlantic Coast Express' between Bude and Exeter on Friday 14 August 1964. It was withdrawn from Eastleigh shed on 3 October 1965, but stored there until February 1966, when it was towed to South Wales and scrapped by Buttigiegs at Newport in March 1966.

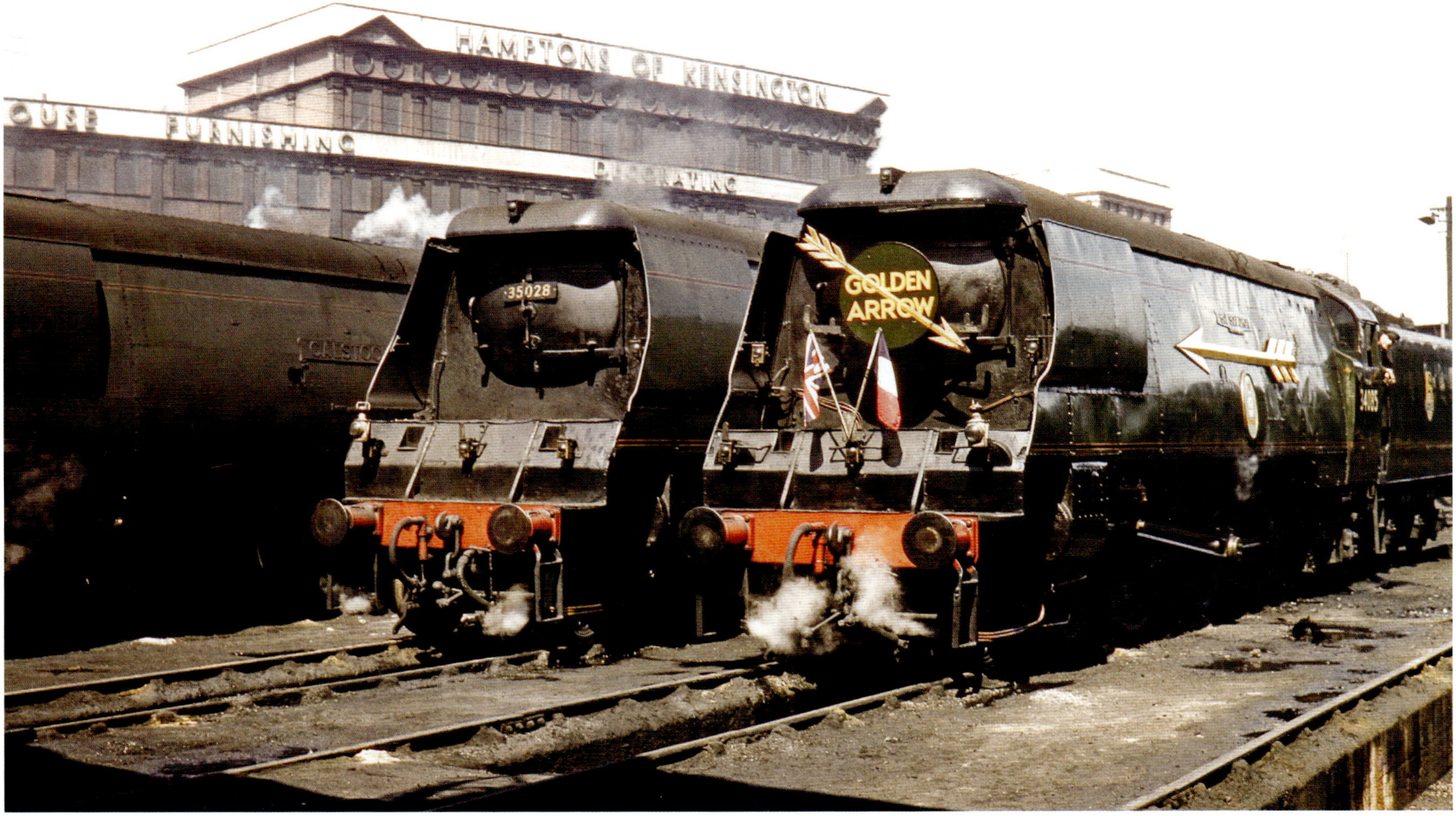
HAMPTONS OF KENSINGTON
FURNISHING
35028
GOLDEN ARROW

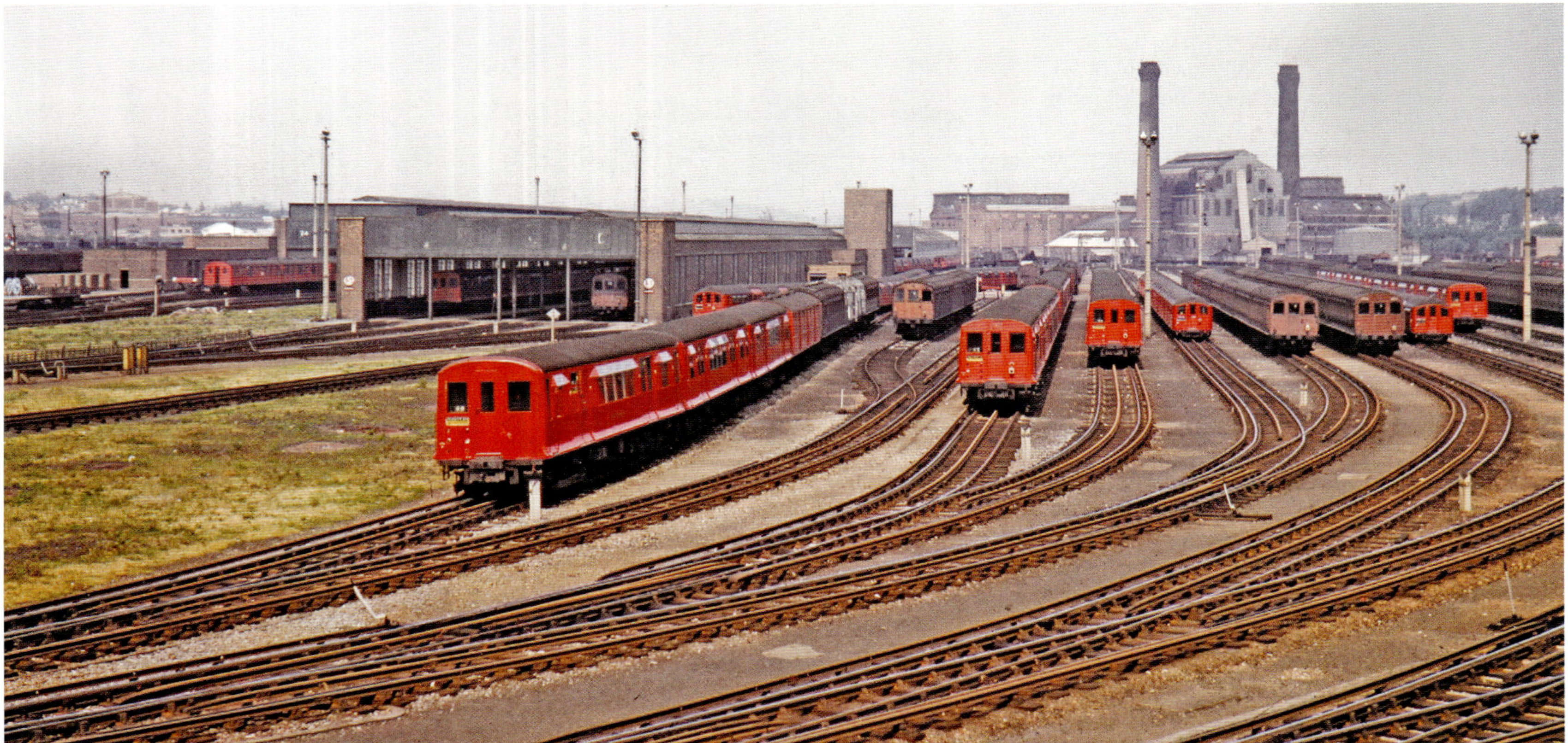

TOP LEFT Three Bulleid engines stand together at Stewarts Lane (Battersea) on 16 August 1959. Furthest away is No 34103 *Calstock* in an everyday grimy condition. At the time the engine was based at Dover, so was here being serviced before working home. With the advancement of the Kent Coast electrification it was transferred to Bournemouth in January 1961 and finally Eastleigh in September 1964, from where it ended its working career a year later. Next is celebrity engine No 35028 *Clan Line*, seen in original condition before rebuilding. At the time based at 'The Lane', this engine was purchased out of service when withdrawn in 1967 and has since become one of the most regular and reliable performers on main-line tours in the ensuing fifty-plus years. Finally comes No 34085 *501 Squadron*, also seen at its home depot and once more prior to rebuilding. The engine is ready and prepared for the prestige 'Golden Arrow' service from Victoria and, like its immediate neighbour, has had some attention from the cleaners. In the background the structure of the furniture depository is a familiar sight and may be seen from the main line out of Waterloo – which passes hard by the other side of the building.

BELOW LEFT In this grand view of the London Transport depot at Neasden in 1957 the power station is in the background. Other than a date of '1957' we are not told when the view was taken, but a guess could well be outside peak times, as witness the number of units stabled. Points to note are the variety of sets together with their physical stature – to suit the sizes of the particular lines, usually those operating on the deeper 'tubes' being the smaller – the overall red colour of all the trains, although sometimes it is perhaps intentionally more maroon, and the universal use of oil tail lamps. (British Railways was still doing likewise until the early to mid-1960s, even with electric and diesel trains.) Several different types of set are visible including O/P, T, and 1938 stock. No doubt lurking in the bowels of the shed or in some almost hidden siding there may well have been some odd relics waiting to be found! Most of the track is electrified on the fourth-rail principle, although one siding in the centre may be noted where electricity is not present.

RIGHT An unidentified 'Grange' leaves Truro with a down train – towards Penzance – on 13 July 1955. All four coaches are in Western Region 'chocolate and cream' livery, and the first three vehicles at least are Mk 1 stock (and from the periscope roof lookouts probably the fourth as well.). Slightly unusual is the 'A' 'express' headcode carried by the engine, especially as it is such a short working, but I am sure that there must be a perfectly logical explanation! In the left background are the lines leading to Truro engine shed, a dead-end shed with six stabling roads and a repair line between the two groups of three; this also goes to explain the number of engines in the area. Most of the yard and goods facilities were on the north of the main line, as seen here, while the passenger station had three through platforms and a bay for down trains. 'West' signal box is also visible. The 'Grange' displays the first BR emblem on the tender and has just passed the down starting signal, the stop arm of which is 'off' but the distant is 'on'. The 'chocolate and cream' livery for rolling stock used on the principal passenger services had started to be seen again from about 1953, while regional autonomy also meant that soon afterwards Swindon would yet again display its independence by painting almost all steam engines green, despite this supposedly being reserved for the principal passenger classes.

TOP LEFT One of the '15xx' pannier tanks, number not known, is seen on exactly the duty for which they were intended – carriage shunting and pilot work at Paddington – some time in 1959. Unfortunately it is not possible to discern exactly which engine this is, a pity as generally images of the class are certainly not as common as other classes. The location is close to Westbourne Park and the engine will shortly enter a platform with its train, which will have been serviced at nearby Old Oak – separate areas were set aside for the locomotive depot and for the carriage sidings. As referred to earlier, we also have examples of all three rolling stock paint schemes that were around from the early to late 1950s onwards: the early 'crimson and cream', also known rather cruelly as 'blood and custard', 'chocolate and cream', and, in the background, maroon. The coach in the background is a suburban non-corridor vehicle; these were made up into rakes and used on the outer-suburban services hauled by '61xx' tank engines – that is, until all such workings were turned over to DMUs.

There were only ten members in the '15xx' class, with four based in South Wales. Built by BR in 1949, they were victims of modernisation and were generally consigned to scrap long before they were truly life-expired, consequently it was not surprising when three, Nos 1501, 1502 and 1509, were sold out of service to the National Coal Board for use at Coventry, but sent first to Messrs Andrew Barclay in Kilmarnock for overhaul. They continued to work for the NCB until 1970 when all three were sold to the Severn Valley Railway. No 1501 was restored using the other two engines as donors of spares, after which the cannibalised pair were scrapped by an outside contractor. No 1501 has been a regular and popular performer on the SVR for many years since 1970.

BOTTOM LEFT This image from the collection has a particular appeal. This is Launceston (GWR side) with No 4549 being turned by hand – presumably by the fireman – while the driver 'sweats it out' in the cab. No 4549 will likely have worked down from Plymouth and is being returned ready for the journey home. It is May 1960, and while the engine displays the brackets on the smokebox door for a BR numberplate, this is missing and a GWR style of painted number has been reapplied to the front buffer beam. Likely No 4549 has also not had a repaint for some time – certainly the old style of BR crest remains on the tank side. It is typical of the smaller 'Prairie' tanks working the line, and in the eyes of many also more visually appealing than the later '4575' series, which had sloping tops to the side tanks. It is seen here 'nicely weathered' – well, it did have 45 years service to its credit. This, though, would be its swansong, its last full year in service, as it was withdrawn at the end of 1961, a year before services from Plymouth to Launceston via the GWR line also ceased to operate.

Launceston was the end of the GWR route, but there was also a junction with the former LSWR line from Halwill Junction (south of Okehampton) to Wadebridge and Padstow. Each company maintained its own part of the station, with two engine sheds, two turntables and indeed two independent routes to Plymouth. From June 1952 old rivalries were set aside and passenger services were concentrated at the former SR facilities.

ABOVE Where 'Duchesses' passed at speed – well, in one direction at least – times could occasionally also be somewhat more leisurely. Such is the case here with former Caledonian Railway 'Standard Passenger' design tank engine No 55232 at Beattock station in 1958. The 0-4-4 tank engine could well be in charge of a train to or from the freight-only line to Moffat, which lost its passenger service in 1954, yet continued to handle goods for a further decade. Appropriate also as Beattock had been on the former Caledonian Railway system. Sixty-nine members of the class were on the books of BR in 1951, but that number gradually dwindled and by 1962 just seven were active. All, including No 55232 seen here, had gone by the end of the year, although one of the survivors, No 55189, is fortunately preserved. Notice too the builder's plate at the base of the bunker.

Here is the unmistakable vista of the steam shed at Whitemoor, Cambridgeshire, or March (31B) as it was also known. In the background is the control tower of the hump yard, which at its peak could accommodate more than 17,000 wagons. March shed was built by the Great Eastern Railway as part of the redevelopment of local railway facilities in the mid-1880s, when the construction of a new, larger station at March had meant that the earlier engine shed had had to be demolished. Construction of the new shed included realigning the branch line to Wisbech further west and replacing a level crossing at Norwood Road with a bridge. The new shed was a brick-built six-track straight shed with a triple gable-style slate roof. The two northernmost roads were through lines and the other four were dead ends on the west side. In 1900 a turntable was provided on the north side of the shed yard, being enlarged to a 70-foot diameter in 1925, the same time as a corrugated asbestos-clad four-track straight-through shed was added along the north side of the original building.

After the 1923 Grouping the London & North Eastern Railway built a new locomotive shed in Hundred Road with a Mitchell Conveyor & Transporter Co mechanical coaling plant (seen on the right) for the engines, and an associated electricity generating plant. The entire line had became part of the Great Eastern Railway in 1862 and the former GER engine shed was retained to undertake heavy repairs. A brick-built five-track straight-through washout shed was added in 1933. A water softener with a capacity of 11,700 gallons per hour was added in 1939, at a cost of more than £12,000.

March shed was considered of strategic importance at both operational and national level. The LNER diesel-electric shunters, locomotives that included a large switching board at the rear of the cab to enable them to be used as mobile power stations in the event of bomb damage affecting local supplies, were delivered new to the shed. Due to locomotive examination problems caused by the wartime blackout, the shed was provided with an illuminated loco inspection pit, generally referred to as the 'Light Tunnel'. This building contained six rows of tube lights, two on either wall and one on either side of the pit, and remained in use until the end of steam. During the Second World War in 1943 and 1944 a number of US Army 'S160' Class 2-8-0s were allocated to the shed in the run-up to the invasion of Europe, and at the time of nationalisation 199 engines were allocated to the depot.

RIGHT Taken on 14 May 1959, when Roy enjoyed a footplate ride on No 70000 (although it also might have been No 70002, on which he also rode on the same day), this is the fireman's view from the cab as the 'Britannia' passes (we think) Hall Farm Junction en route to/from Ipswich. Alongside are two small 0-6-0 diesel shunting engines; that on the right in black livery is No 11128, built by Messrs Drewry in 1955 and later renumbered as D2222, which lasted in service until 1968. In green alongside is a 1957-built 0-6-0 in the 'D204'(?) series. Both were rated at 204hp. It appears that a third machine is lurking inside the shed.

BELOW RIGHT Replacement for steam on the Eastern Region, Brush Type 2 (later Class 31) No D5504 is seen at Stratford on 30 March 1958, exactly two months after entering service. This class – sister engine D5500 just creeps into the view alongside – was one of the Pilot Scheme diesel classes ordered as part of the BR Modernisation Plan, with the first of the design, D5500, completed in September 1957. In all, 163 were eventually built in two batches and took the numbers D5500-99 and D5800-62. The first twenty were fitted with 1,250hp engines, while later locos had 1,365hp power units. Neither were particularly good and, after a successful trial in 1964, the entire class was retro-fitted with a 1,470hp engine. As time progressed so changes to the design and equipment occurred. For example, the first twenty were not fitted with a rooftop headcode box and so gained the unfortunate nickname of 'Skinheads'. Other less than pleasing designations were 'Gurglers', as a result of the noise from the engine, or 'Toffee Apples', from the shape of the control handle. When new the class was allocated to the Eastern Region and took over secondary passenger, parcels and freight work from steam. Later the locos' sphere of operation increased and they could be seen on most of the former BR regions, although one Southern man was heard to remark, 'They would not pull the skin off a rice pudding.' Notwithstanding, several survived into the 21st century and a few are still operational on the national network, albeit mechanically and electrically heavily modified from the original design.

There were many variations of mechanical ground signals on the railways in the days before remote operation from power boxes changed these to light indications. Here we see ground signals at West Thurrock Junction on 23 March 1957; both are 'stop' signals, meaning that the driver must not pass them unless one had moved upwards to an angle of between 45° and 60°. The two signals one above the other applied to two different routes with the simple rule 'Top to bottom, left to right', meaning that the topmost signal was for the line furthest over to the left. Of course the driver would need to have route knowledge and know where he was heading. Both signals are oil-lit, likely having to be refilled every 24 hours or so by the local lampman, who would carry out a similar task at all the mechanical signals in his area. The two arms have had many applications of paint over the years, although time has taken its toll and the red is a now a more subtle shade of pink in places.

Ken Nunn, well-known enthusiast and photographer and member of the Locomotive Club of Great Britain, is enjoying a brake van trip at Dunmow during what is thought to have been a private trip some time in July 1957. Mr Nunn was a fan of all things railway, particularly Great Eastern, but also a prolific photographer and collector of material. His photographic collection is now with the National Railway Museum at York. These were the times when it was possible to arrange such trips (and visits to railway premises) either for a group or even as an individual. Indeed, your author recalls being offered a brake van trip between Newbury and Welford Park in 1971 for the princely sum of £5.00, the amount to cover the cost of an Inspector who would have to be present. Unfortunately the funds of an impoverished student prevented me from taking up the offer, something that has been regretted ever since as it of course now totally impossible to replicate the chance.

Commencing in 1956, London Transport purchased thirteen former GWR pannier tanks for use on overground lines. Their purpose was for engineers' trains and none were ever used on passenger service. Based at either Lillie Bridge or Neasden, they replaced older LT steam engines and would survive to be the final steam type operating on LT, the last not taken out of service until 1971. With the demise of steam they became ever more popular with enthusiasts and were even the subject of a letter to *The Times* when a north London resident wrote to enquire about what he had imagined to be the sound of steam locomotive, yet had believed that such things had been consigned for scrap years past! During their lifetime major repairs were carried out away from LT, and several are known to have visited Eastleigh on occasions.

Seen here is the first. BR(W) No 7711 from 1930 and purchased by LT in 1956. This machine was in need of repairs in 1961, but they were not considered worthwhile and in consequence it was scrapped, being replaced by another pannier tank, former BR No 7760, also from 1930. The replacement was given the same L90 number and was one of the last three in service in 1971, being sold out of service to 7029 Clun Castle Ltd. Apart from a smart change of livery, other modifications so that the engines could work on LT lines were made to the cab, and the fitting of tripcock brake valves. It is interesting to note that the purchase of these particular steam engines had come about after a former GNR 'J52' type had been rejected, together with a fleet of diesel shunters, although it would be three diesel-hydraulic shunters that would eventually oust the steam fleet in 1971. The original No L90 is seen with a proud engineman at Neasden on 1 June 1957.

LSWR 'O2' 0-4-4T No 30192, on a Calstock and Callington train, waits at the branch platform at Bere Alston in June 1960. Little would have probably changed in this scene for many years; the 'O2' Class and LSWR 'gate-stock' had been in use likely since the 1930s, although in a different livery back then, of course. The single-track branch trundled its way downhill and made a sharp turn across the viaduct carrying the railway over the Tamar. On the right are sidings laid on more level ground, and containing spare passenger stock as well as a goodly supply of vans for the soft fruit traffic that emanated from the branch stations at this time of year. On the extreme left the main line is that from Plymouth, northwards via the LSWR route through Okehampton to Exeter – in the 21st century this has been reduced to a stub from the Plymouth direction, but still fortunately serves much of the original Callington branch, both now referred to as 'rural railways'. In this 1960s view the whole was still very much part of the main network, as witness the signals, the starting and advanced starting both on rail-built posts, while the home signal has a wooden post. One can almost smell the dust, old varnish and old smoke that would been trapped in the saloon, and feel the harshness of the sprung seats. No air-conditioning of course – anything like that was achieved by simply opening the windows!

Back to earlier times now with 'L1' 2-6-4T No 67713 at Liverpool Street in June 1948, resplendent in LNER Apple Green with a BR number and ownership identification written in full. Despite what might at first be thought, this was actually the first livery carried by this engine as it had not entered traffic until 1 April 1948, so was just two months old when photographed. Designs from the four pre-nationalisation companies continued to be built well into BR days; indeed, the numbers involved are considerable and when combined total far more than the number of BR Standard types constructed. For completeness, the figures are: LNER type – 396, between 1948 and 1952; LMS type – 640, between 1948 and 1954; SR type – 50, between 1948 and 1951; and GWR type – 452, between 1948 and 1956. In all cases these were from a variety of classes. Combined, this makes a total of 1,538 new steam engines added to stock between 1948 and 1956; add this to the 999 new 'Standard' steam engines introduced between 1951 and 1960 and we have a quite amazing figure of 2,537, none of which would have a life exceeding 20 years, and in many cases just single figures. What is perhaps most amazing of all is that the WR was still receiving engines to pre-nationalisation designs in 1956, a full year after the Modernisation Plan had been announced forecasting the end of steam traction. No 67713 would survive for thirteen years and was withdrawn from Cambridge at the end of October 1961, after which it was moved to Darlington Works, coincidentally the same place where it had been built, to be cut up there at the end of January 1962.

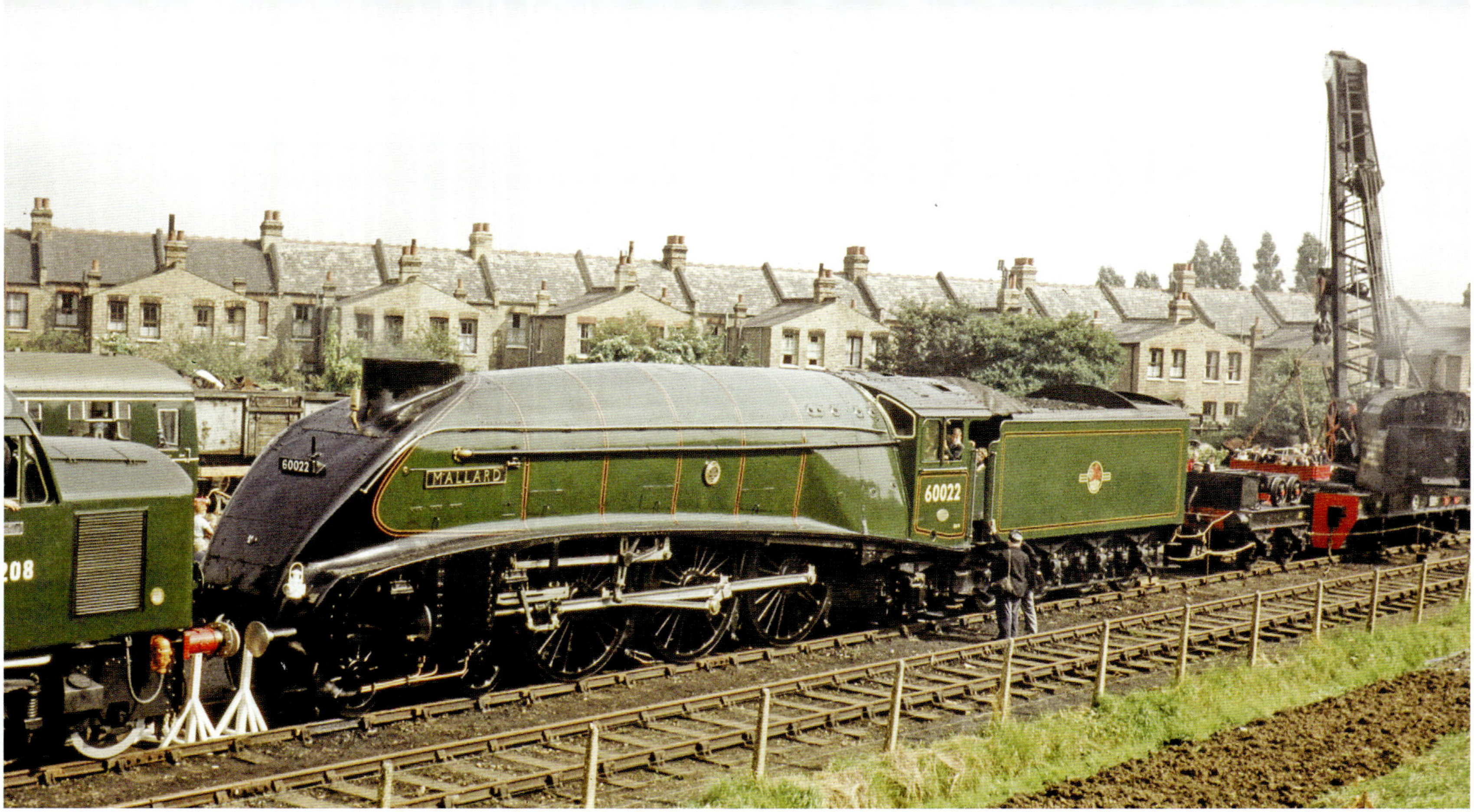
60022
MALLARD
60022
208

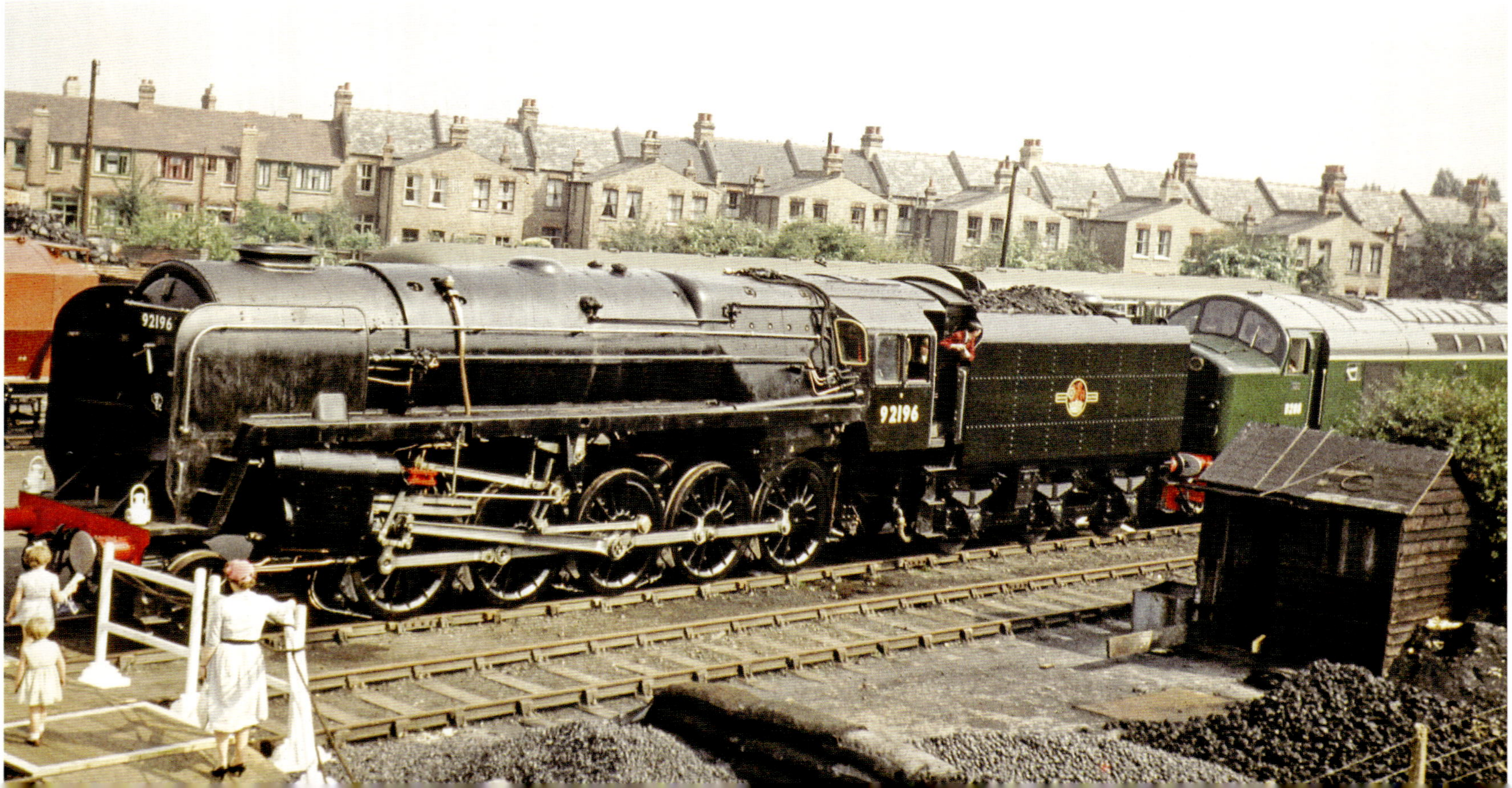
92196
92196

OPPOSITE AND RIGHT Over the three days from Friday to Sunday 12 to 14 September 1958 an exhibition was held at Noel Green goods depot to celebrate the Charter Celebrations of the Borough of Wood Green. A total of 14,000 people attended to view the 41 exhibits, which were 'A4' No 60022 *Mallard*, 9F No 92196, 'J52' No 68846, 'C12' No 67352, diesels Nos D208, D5300 and D3490, and two diesel railcars, Nos E52161 and E56419. Other exhibits were a cinema coach, sleeping cars, the Peterborough breakdown crane and various freight wagons. A special diesel service was provided from Hitchin to reach the location. Visitors could also climb into the cabs of the various locomotive exhibits. Something that was normal with some events – and such exhibitions were relatively common at the time – was the way the public were also 'involved' – literally. In the background to the view of No 60022, the Peterborough steam crane, No 110, will be noticed; look carefully and it can be seen to have chains around an open wagon that the public were invited to enter and which would then be lifted into the air to give those inside an aerial view of proceedings. 'Health & Safety'? Well, there are no reports of anyone falling out…

North Eastern Railway design 0-6-0T No 68700 shunts the yard at Keith some time during its tenure at that depot, which ended with its withdrawal at the end of 1958. Keith itself was on the former Great North of Scotland Railway route from Aberdeen, and formed an end-on connection with the Highland Railway line from Inverness. At Keith the Great North of Scotland also turned south-west through Keith Town, continuing until it met up again with another HR route at Boat of Garten. This was obviously a visit of some sort, and it is unfortunate that the wording on the red oval disc placed on the top lamp bracket of No 68700 cannot be read. Prominent are the two wooden-bodied wagons immediately behind the engine, the design of such vehicles dating back many decades.

Still in Scotland and some 29 miles west of Keith, LMS 'Black 5' No 45319 shunts a decidedly ancient wooden-framed open wagon at Forres in April 1957. Undoubtedly one of the most universally popular engine types, the class could be seen literally anywhere from Scotland to the South Coast, and might even stray occasionally on to the Western and Eastern Regions. No fewer than 842 were built to the design of William Stanier from 1934 onwards, the last taking to the rails in 1951. Such was their popularity and indeed longevity – members of the type were active until the very last days of steam on BR in August 1968 – that eighteen of the class are preserved. No 45319 seen here was built by the contractor Armstrong Whitworth in 1937, one of 559 engines that company built for UK railways. It survived for thirty years and was withdrawn in May 1967, thus not reaching the milepost of the end of steam. It was destined not to be saved and was despatched by J. McWilliams at Shettleston.

Here is an 'auto-train' working in Cornwall (it was never 'push-pull' on the Western!). No specific location, date or locomotive details are known, but dealing with the first we think it is the rebuilt Coldrennick Viaduct, between St Germans and Liskeard, and if so is 795 feet in length. As with many similar structures on the original Cornwall Railway, it had once been one of Brunel's timber viaducts and was originally erected in 1857. After a life of forty-one years it was replaced in 1898 with a new upper structure as seen, but retaining the original piers – several of the viaducts were built on new piers erected alongside the originals and these may still be seen today. Unusually, at Coldrennick the replacement structure was not a series of arches but instead girder sections. The date cannot be accurately guessed, but the locomotive is either a '54xx' or '64xx' pannier tank with three auto-coaches likely of 59-foot length. The driver will be at the leading end of the coach controlling the regulator, brake and a foot-operated bell in lieu of the train whistle. Communication with the fireman was via a series of bell codes as, in addition to his normal duty of tending to the fire and boiler, he was also expected to shorten or lengthen the cut-off as required. The GWR and its successor the Western Region continued to operate auto-trains of this type on numerous branch lines until the demise of steam in the mid-1960s. Generally the system worked well, although the mechanical operation of the regulator could be problematical if the linkage was stiff, a problem often accentuated on sharp curves. For this reason the maximum number of vehicles was restricted to four – two on either side of the engine. Auto-coaches were of necessity also non-corridor, which meant that the guard, who on some services would also issue tickets, had to move from vehicle to vehicle at the various stops. All auto-coaches were also single-ended, so the train was made up with the driver's end ready for travel. The opposite end of each car was in later years plated over, although originally glass panels had been provided; this arrangement was changed as the glass would regularly break if a lump of coal became dislodged from the engine bunker during the journey.

Swindon-built 'Warship' No D808 *Centaur* calls at Brent in Devon between Totnes and Plymouth on 17 May 1960. Opened circa 1848, there was a station here until October 1964, and from 1848 to 1963 it was also the junction for the 12-mile branch line running almost due south to Kingsbridge. On the May day when this image was taken a westbound service has arrived at the down platform and is making a connection with the branch train, which waits in the bay on the right. The branch train formed a shuttle service to the branch terminus, calling at the intermediate stations of Avonwick, Gara Bridge and Loddiswell (a proposed extension from Kingsbridge to Salcombe was never built). For most of its life the Kingsbridge branch was steam-operated and certainly for fifty years at least was in the hands of 'small Prairie'-type engines; only in its last days did the throb of a DMU engine intrude, and that was deemed insufficient to forestall closure after what was a bitter and hard-fought campaign that left many open wounds. With the branch no more there was little justification for the station at Brent, and BR would shed no tears at the prospect of eastbound trains no longer having to stop on the stiff climb of the south Devon banks.

The photograph here could almost be timeless – save for the motive power and paint styles, of course. We are not told the train, but the two discs indicate an 'A' class (express) working (train types were identified by discs on all regions except the Southern, where the discs indicated the route instead). In the yard is a variety of goods stock including one of the instantly recognised 'Toad'-type brake vans. In addition to the passenger platforms there are two loops, one through the goods shed and another running across the far right. Slightly unusual are the two catchpoints in the turnout leading to the first goods siding, while the position of the stop signal on the exit road from the goods shed is also uncommon.

LEFT Battery Electric Locomotive No 1 (B.E.L. No 1) is seen at Poplar Docks on 5 May 1956. Built by the Midland Railway at Derby in 1913, it could produce 82hp and was fitted with two traction motors – presumably one per axle, as the axles were not coupled. A very similar machine, B.E.L. 2, followed from the North Staffordshire Railway at Stoke in 1917 (Wikipedia also quotes 1914 as the build date), and both are believed to have been constructed on the underframes of former four-wheel wagons. Despite its almost unique status, No 1 spent its BR days shunting at Poplar until scrapped in 1964. No 2, however, was saved and today forms part of the National Collection. The engine weighed in the order of 18 tons, most of which was the weight of the battery, but that would have still given it a reasonable amount of pull when moving a wagon or two on dry rails. In wet conditions things might have been different, but then it would never have survived were it not considered fit for purpose. Notice that the machine (we have some slight difficulty in referring to it as a 'locomotive', although to be fair that indeed was what it was) had sand boxes fitted. In the background are a number of still devastated buildings from the time of the London Blitz.

RIGHT Inside the famous 'A' Shop at Swindon Works 'Hall' No 5911 *Preston Hall* is in the course of overhaul and rub-down prior to repainting on 16 June 1957. No 5911 was built at Swindon in 1931 to Lot No 275, which covered twenty engines of the class taking the running numbers 5901 to 5920; all entering service between May and August 1931. This was a 'Heavy General' repair for No 5911, and the last it would ever receive, although there were several other periods of subsequent, lesser, maintenance during its life. At the same time, June 1957, the engine was paired with a replacement tender – for the record, tender No 2807. Of particular interest are the number of components in the foreground, which primarily appear to be eccentrics and other valve gear parts. Likely the chalked numbers also refer to the specific locomotive they are from or destined for.

Swindon Works would close it doors in the mid-1980s, a hurtful decision that was only partly smoothed when a Japanese car manufacturer opened its own engineering plant on the outskirts of the town. Today the works site serves a new purpose: no longer does the repair and building of rolling stock and locomotives take place, but instead there are homes, offices, a large shopping centre and of course the excellent STEAM Museum, some of these utilising the old works buildings, many of which fortunately have listed status. No 5911 would also not survive, although other members of the 342-strong 'Hall' Class did; instead it was withdrawn at the end of September 1962 from Cardiff Canton shed and cut up fourteen months later at Bridgend, having run just over 1.2 million miles in service.

The charm of the rural railway is typified here at Midhurst, West Sussex, in May 1950. Of the three persons visible, at least two are railwaymen, hardly sufficient to cover operating costs, let alone provide a profit. Midhurst was originally the junction for three lines. A route east from Petersfield operated by the LSWR ran to its own station in the town. Next came a line west from Harham Junction near Pulborough, which reached the LBSCR station seen here. Finally a connection was made from the LBSCR running south to Chichester. Changes began in 1925 when the Southern Railway closed the former LSWR station and concentrated all operations on the LBSCR site, a former link between the two that had only been used for goods exchange being upgraded for passenger work. Then in the 1930s passenger services ceased south to Chichester, although when this photograph was taken the line was still in use for goods, although this would come to an abrupt halt at the end of 1951 when a bridge wash-out occurred between Midhurst and the first station south at Cocking. Passenger services between Petersfield and Midhurst and also from Pulborough to Midhurst ceased in February 1955, the Petersfield line closing completely at the same time. Goods from Pulborough lingered on for almost another decade, although now the site has been redeveloped and it is likely that few who live in the town today would know that it had once possessed two stations and three different routes. Seen in the Petersfield bay is an 'M7' and 'pull-push' set No 732; on the right is the main station, which had two platforms, looking towards Petworth and Pulborough.

The 'modern' railway (well, it was then, but with old signalling) is represented by a pair of BR-built 4-SUB units headed by set No 4678 passing Chelsfield on a down Charing Cross to Sevenoaks working on 10 May 1952. The term 'SUB' referred to 'Suburban' and was first used in 1941 to refer to newly built sets. The Southern Railway and later the Southern Region eventually had more than 500 of these four-car units in use, and many of the earlier units, which varied somewhat in external appearance, were augmented from three to four cars as passenger numbers increased. In what was typical Southern Railway/Region style, most of the 1949-51 build, of which set No 4678 was one, were constructed with new bodies on old frames, each set consisting of a pair of Driving Motor Brake Trailer Opens at each end with two identical non-corridor vehicles sandwiched between. Conditions could become cramped to say the least, and 'cosy', if not ripe, on a warm day, so small wonder that the daily commute came to be regarded as a chore. On the opposite line the signals are what is referred to as 'co-acting', which means that the top signal is provided to enable its aspect to be seen at a greater distance, as the lower arm alone might otherwise be obstructed by a station canopy or other structure. Both arms move simultaneously and are of the upper-quadrant type. Finally notice the '8' board just visible on the concrete post: this was to indicate to the driver where he should stop if his train consisted of … eight coaches. Latterly referred to as 'slam-door' stock, the last of the SUB units were withdrawn from service in 1983.

A relic from a past age, this London & North Western Railway Ramsbottom 0-6-0ST 'Special tank' was photographed at Crewe Works on 19 March 1960. Introduced from 1870 onwards, five of the class managed to survive into BR ownership, all being used as shunting engines at former LMS works. Three, Nos CD3, 6 and 7 – the latter seen here – were allocated to the carriage works at Wolverton. No CD7 was withdrawn from service in 1959 at the ripe old age of 81. It had originally carried a brass plate 'Carr Dept Wol No.7', but this was removed and is now in the care of the National Railway Museum. Behind is the tramway engine described earlier.

From a design of 1870 to one of 1951, British Railways-built 'Britannia' Class No 70003 *John Bunyan* at Old Bishopsgate just outside Liverpool Street in July 1958. Electrification of the suburban services out of Liverpool Street is present in this view and while steam is clearly in decline it was still the motive power for the longer-distance trains to and from the terminus. Behind the tender is a variety of coaching stock, some BR standard coaches and certainly also some former LNER vehicles. The 'Britannia' is not quite in original condition, having had the handrails on the smoke deflectors replaced by handholds in direct consequence of the Didcot derailment of 1955, when it was considered that the driver's view ahead may have been obstructed by the handrails located almost at eye-level. As a consequence changes were made first to the Western Region allocation of the type, then later elsewhere. No 70003, the fourth member of the class, was new from Crewe Works on 1 March 1951 and was allocated to Stratford for Great Eastern line services at the end of the same month. It stayed there until moving to Norwich Thorpe in February 1959, then March in August 1959. It transferred from the Eastern to the London Midland Region in November 1963, being sent to Carlisle Kingmoor, where it ended its days withdrawn from service in March 1967. Eight months later it was reduced to scrap.

Most of the time photographers concentrated their camera on locomotives, trains and to a lesser extent stations. Infrastructure was invariably neglected, yet here we have a record of a provision that existed at almost every station, depot or yard – the humble fire bucket. Three seemed to be the average number (was this a regulatory requirement?) and as recalled might contain water or sand; the railways were wise to the comment that not all fires might be successfully extinguished using water. The local station master, or person in charge, was responsible for seeing that the water was kept topped up and that in winter ice not allowed to form; this task, like the winding of the station clock (another requirement at stations), was invariably delegated to the junior porter. Buckets containing sand also had to be refreshed when necessary and cleared of their own collection of combustibles – usually 'fag-ends' and perhaps bits of paper – that might otherwise accumulate and have the opposite effect if the contents were needed in emergency.

At Midford on the Somerset & Dorset line, where this view was taken on 9 July 1960, we can assume that all was 'according to the rules', the staff here proud of their station and keen to ensure that it was always presented in a good light. Unfortunately that would not be enough to ensure its survival, and Midford, together with the whole of the 71-mile former Somerset & Dorset Joint line from Bath to Bournemouth, closed in March 1966. (Roy's original image was taken at a slight angle, which we have deliberately straightened – otherwise it could be said there might have been the risk of the contents of the buckets spilling out…)

In deepest Cornwall one of the almost antique Beattie 'Well Tanks', No 30585, cautiously approaches an ungated road crossing on 14 July 1960, no doubt accompanied by judicious amounts of whistling. (Notice the shunter's pole lying across the front buffer beam.) Like the Adams 4-4-2T class seen earlier on the Lyme Regis branch, the Beattie 'Well Tanks' were a throwback to an earlier age, eighty-five engines having been built between 1863 and 1875 for use on suburban trains out of Waterloo. Their tenure, though, was brief, and all but three had gone by the start of the 20th century, including thirty-one of the type that had been converted to tender engines. The three survivors now found a use on the Bodmin & Wadebridge Railway, one of the earliest in Cornwall, which was isolated from the rest of the LSWR system until 1895. From that time on, and for the next sixty-seven, years they worked the sharply curved Wenford Bridge freight line, which was a branch of the B&W, until finally replaced by former GWR 0-6-0 dock tanks, themselves having been made redundant due to dieselisation. Before their demise, though, the 'Well Tanks' had a brief swansong on railtour duty around the London area, and two of the three are preserved, No 30585 is one of them, now owned by the Quainton Railway Society and based at its Buckinghamshire Railway Centre.

On 2 May 1959 Brunel's Royal Albert Bridge across the Tamar west of Plymouth reached its centenary. Sometimes known as the Saltash bridge due to the village, and station, of that name being hard by the western end, Saltash celebrated the day with flags and bunting; there was even a special train from Paddington to mark the occasion. The bridge is single track and understandably subject to an speed limit, allowing ample time to observe a train passing – such as here, with what appears to be a 'Hall' making its way across attached to a mixed rake of BR and former GWR stock, which includes a 70-foot 'Toplight' Brake 3rd. Running across the top of the spans may be seen a handrail, a necessary provision for the men working on the bridge – it can get quite windy up there. Before this was provided there existed a small 'guard-rail' literally no more than 2-3 inches high, intended to warn the men should their feet stray. In reality this was more of a trip hazard than a safety feature. Today the bridge still stands serving its original purpose of taking trains to and from Cornwall, although it is perhaps slightly overshadowed with the A38 dual-carriageway road bridge from the 1960s running alongside.

ABOVE No 6824 *Ashley Grange* is coaled and ready to go at Plymouth Laira in June 1956. Despite the obvious family resemblance between the various Great Western classes of tender engine, the 'Grange' Class could always be easily identified by the raised footplating above the cylinders, on account of their smaller wheel diameter of 5ft 8in compared with the 'Hall' Class at 6 feet, and the 'Castles' at 6ft 8½in. According to some footplatemen, the 'Grange' was the best class of tender engine there was, able to run fast if required – perhaps not quite up to the normal 'Castle' maximum of 90mph, but equally able to haul prodigious loads.

No 6824 is seen here attached to a 4,000-gallon tender, although some of the class might also to be seen with tenders of smaller capacity. In the background the red van belongs to the Laira Breakdown Train and is fitted out as a staff riding and messing vehicle. No 6824 was at the time based at Penzance, so is likely ready for its return working over the 80-odd-mile route. New from Swindon in January 1937, it moved sheds to Laira, albeit briefly, in August 1962. By this time, though, dieselisation was almost complete in Cornwall, so it was soon on its way again, this time to Didcot in October 1962. Again its tenure was limited and it moved to Oxford in November 1963, being withdrawn from there in April 1964 and meeting its end at Swindon Works dump likely towards the end of the same year.

TOP RIGHT Taken slightly earlier than the pervious view of Brent – the 'Warship' diesel that featured can just be seen poking its nose under the footbridge – 'small Prairie' No 5558 is reversing to run round its train following arrival from Kingsbridge, ready to attach to the front of the coaches in the bay and form the next departure down the branch. However, note that the only way through that is clear is via the goods shed, so No 5558 will proceed that way, taking care that it does not catch out an unwary goods porter or clerk! Meanwhile the down starting signal is 'off', its short post enabling the position of the arm to be seen from under the footbridge. There is also a telephone cabinet hard by the base of the signal, which could be used to communicate directly with the station signal box should a train be held at the signal for any length of time or when shunting. No 5558 carries the 'local passenger train' headcode of one lamp below the chimney, although spare lamps were also always carried, and these can just be made out on the right-hand framing in front of the steam pipe. Today all of this has been swept away. No longer are there any 'Warship' diesels or 'small Parries' operating, while the rolling stock has also been superseded, just like Brent station itself; indeed, few if any passengers will give even a glance as they speed past in their 21st-century trains.

BOTTOM RIGHT We now go north again to Scotland and the former Highland Railway station at Forres, junction for the line down to Aviemore. Here at the locomotive shed we see an example of a 1906-built Macintosh '439' or 'Standard Passenger' Class tank engine, having more than a passing resemblance to the 0-4-4T engine depicted at Beattock earlier. Several railway companies were building engines of this type at this period, as witness the 'M7' and smaller 'O2' types of the LSWR, also recorded earlier. Forres was a small depot coming under the control of Inverness and usually had an allocation of only about four engines; the shed closed on 31 May 1959. No 55178 looks in good external order and was smartly lined out when photographed in the shed yard on 20 April 1957. Slightly unusual is the securing arrangement for the smokebox door, consisting of a wheel and lever instead of the more standard pair of levers, in addition to which two clamps are also provided at the bottom. The engine is both vacuum-braked and Westinghouse air-braked, and lasted in service until the last day of 1958.

BELOW Top Shed at King's Cross was where, in steam days, locomotives were prepared for duty on main-line workings, and arriving engines were serviced before their return north. In this view two of the stalwart types from the days of steam are visible. On the left is the unmistakable outline of an 'A4', represented by No 60026 *Miles Beevor*, then there are two 'A3s', Nos 60066 *Merry Hampton* and 60047 *Donovan*. All three carry the local '34A' shed code, and are ready for duty in September 1961, perhaps not quite as clean as they once were but still with some life left, although their main-line replacements, the 'Deltic' diesels, were knocking on the door ready to take over. In consequence steam started to vanish from main-line workings in and out of King's Cross soon after, the diesels being serviced at a newly built depot at Finsbury Park. All three engines would end their days as scrap, to be recycled into – well, whatever. The two 'A3's went first, No 60047 from New England (Peterborough) on 8 April 1963, while No 60066 succumbed at Grantham on 8 September 1963. Note that No 60047 has German-style half smoke deflectors, which were fitted to some members of the 'A3' Class and produced a subjective change so far as aesthetics were concerned; nonetheless their presence appears to have been appreciated by crews in lifting the exhaust steam so allowing greater visibility ahead. Like its two stable mates, No 60026 also moved north, again to New England, where it was deemed redundant and ceased work officially from 21 December 1965.

RIGHT In this undated view, the DMU is coming off the up branch from Wensum Junction at Norwich Thorpe Junction and will head under the bridge into the passenger station at Thorpe. This was a busy signal box of forty levers, and worked with four others. Space constraints have dictated that the signals for the DMU are placed on the opposite side of the line, where both the relevant stop and distant signals are in the 'off' position – the signalman will not restore these to 'on' until the train is clear of all turnouts locked by the signals, even if there are track circuits in the area. A mixture of flat-bottom and bullhead rail may be seen, mostly the latter, and all signals are of the upper-quadrant type.

The DMU is one of the original 'Derby Lightweight' sets with mechanical transmission, introduced in 1954/55. They were the first DMU sets to be built en masse for BR and comprised 217 vehicles formed into two-car sets, with a single or two power cars, and four-car sets. Later one of the powered vehicles in the two-car units was removed to form a single-car unit. The sets were responsible for both increasing traffic and, in some cases, also delaying the closure of some branch lines, although they certainly did not keep the axe from all of them. The trains themselves also showed that the DMU concept was generally a success, and in consequence numerous other types were ordered and delivered from several builders over the following years, as well as from BR workshops themselves. However, being non-standard compared with other sets, the 'Derby Lightweights' had all been withdrawn from normal traffic by 1969. Several survived in departmental service and three vehicles have survived.

LEFT London Transport Peckett-built 0-6-0T No L53 stands at Neasden on 1 June 1957. This engine was already 60 years old when photographed and had originally been Metropolitan Railway No 101. It was one of two identical engines that had consecutive numbers – Metropolitan Nos 101 and 102/LT Nos 53 and 54 – purchased for the specific purpose of shunting at locations such as Finchley Road, Neasden and Harrow. Notwithstanding the influx of former GWR pannier tanks by this time, this engine was still reported as active in 1967. It is painted in what might well be described as an 'oil red' livery – but looks well for it! No vacuum or other brake pipes are fitted, while the coupling is of the three-link type, thus confirming the locomotive's use solely on coal or engineering trains.

British Railways in Unseen Colour: 1948-1962

'O2' No 30225, still active at 69 years of age, is seen here shunting Southern-liveried stock at Laira sidings (Plymouth) on 9 July 1961. This particular machine was seen earlier shunting freight vehicles at Plymouth Friary, and carries a single headcode disc placed to indicate either a Lyme Regis or Exmouth service, although in either case the meaning is likely erroneous and could well instead refer to a local shunt move. The coaching stock is interesting, being a former LNER 3rd Class sleeping car converted during the war as an ambulance car. After the war a number of vehicles from the LNER, LMS and GWR were converted to Cafeteria-type vehicles to cater for the trend away from more formal dining, and that included a pair of former LNER vehicles, now renumbered as S9211E and S9213E. When converted they had carried crimson and cream livery, but were repainted in Southern green in 1956; note also that the panelling that once existed has been plated over. It is very likely that this particular vehicles is No S9213E – we know this as it was photographed by R. C. Riley at the same location on the same date (see *Southern Vans and Coaches in Colour* by Mike King, published by Noodle Books). The Gresley bogies are of a unique type that gave the coach a comfortable ride. Both the Cafeteria cars of this type survived until withdrawn in mid-1963.

Behind is an extremely grubby Bulleid '3-set', while beyond that it is not possible to positively identify what appears to be the last vehicle. The formation had probably been part of a train split at Exeter Central, which then made its way to Plymouth; it will likely return the same way, being attached to other stock at Exeter. In the left background it is just possible to make out the front end of a Western Region 'Castle' Class engine.

Still on the Southern Region, but this time we are on the Isle of Wight at Cowes where pristine 'O2' No W31 *Chale* awaits departure for Newport and Ryde in April 1957. The island members of the class were fitted with an enlarged coal bunker from 1942 onwards, which greatly increased their usefulness as otherwise coal could only be obtained from the two locomotive depots at Newport and Ryde. No W31 has clearly just been in the paint shop at Ryde, as indeed have the coaches – three former LBSCR vehicles – which, like the steam engines, would be used in passenger service until the end of December 1966, long after any similar vehicles had been withdrawn from use on the mainland.

The passenger platforms at Cowes station were on a slight falling gradient towards the buffers, as can be seen when comparing the level of the rails in the coal siding alongside. Here gravity shunting was often resorted to. Once the train had arrived and disgorged its passengers, the engine shunted the coaches back up the platform to clear the engine release crossover seen here. Once the stock was secured, the engine would uncouple and run round, the coaches being allowed to run by gravity towards the buffers. It was an operation that took place for decades without apparent difficulty, and indeed was similar to that at Yelverton described earlier. Today the station at Cowes is no more; passenger services ceased in April 1966 and the site is now occupied by a supermarket. However, the footbridge was saved and, after dismantling, was re-erected at Medstead on the heritage 'Watercress Line'. Sadly that is probably all that survives of this scene; No 31 was one of the last two operational members of the class and, although the fledgling preservation movement wished desperately to see both this and No W24 saved, in the end No 31 went for scrap. Similarly, although some coaches were saved, without being able to identify these specific vehicles it cannot be said if they were among those saved or, like most of the others, were consigned to fire and scrap.

'Meldon-dust-liveried' 'N' Class 2-6-0 No 31836, on a down Plymouth working, approaches Lydford. The 'Meldon dust' reference comes from the grime that would adhere to engines working trains from the quarry of that name just south of Okehampton, and some can even be seen at the far end of the first coach. The train is probably a stopping service between Exeter and Plymouth, calling at all stations.

Of particular interest is the unusual if not unique (certainly unique for the LSWR/Southern in the area) pair of signals on either side of the track. Contrary to appearances, they apply to just one line, the up line from Lydford towards Bridestowe and on towards Okehampton and Exeter. The clue is the curvature of the line at this point, where the normal positioning of the advanced starting signal on the left-hand side of the line was not considered to give the driver of an up train sufficient sighting under bridge No 635, from which the photograph was taken, a particular difficulty for trains that had not called at Lydford. The more normal remedy would have been a co-acting arm – a tall post with two arms, moving together but the upper one able to be seen from afar. Another option where there was a sharp curve was to place the signal on the opposite side of the line, but again this was not considered suitable, nor was a 'banner repeater' provided further back. Hence this unusual arrangement.

Both signals were operated by lever No 31, with the left-hand signal – a delightful lower-quadrant LSWR arm – 506 yards from the signal box around what was a reverse curve from the station. The arm on the post 'planted away from the railway' is even more interesting as it appears to have only a red spectacle and would therefore show either red for stop or white when cleared. This was a throwback to much earlier times when signal indications were red, green or white, green at the time being for caution, later superseded by yellow; in similar fashion the white for 'all clear' was changed to green. The whole gave rise to a rhyme taught to all railwayman of decades past: 'White is right and red is wrong, green means gently go along'. Probably this was the last single-spectacle arm surviving on the Southern Region and it is believed that it remained in use until the route closed in 1968.

ABOVE An artistic perspective: No 5013 *Abergavenny Castle* is seen from between a line of 'lesser' engines at what could be one of the Welsh depots, probably Carmarthen. That on the left is identified as '74xx' No 7439, while that on the right is not confirmed other than to say it is another pannier tank. Pannier tanks were of course the workhorses of the GWR and latterly the Western Region; at their peak there were in the order of 1,000 of several differing types in service, all sharing the 0-6-0 wheel arrangement. Most numerous were the '57xx' series, but there were variations within the class, mainly involving the cab. Then there were the '54xx'/'64xx'/'74xx' series, the '34xx'/'84xx'/'94xx' type, the '15xx' and '1366' Classes and certain older engines of the '2021' series.

In this view the cleaning priority is clearly the passenger engine, the pannier types no doubt mechanically sound but, shall we say, a bit 'grubby around the edges'. Working on steam might have appeared glamorous, but in reality it was dirty, hard work not helped by poor working conditions both on shed and out on the line. Steam had had its day; an engine might only be available for use, say, a maximum of 16 hours a day, and even then the quality of the coal, and ash and clinker, could cause problems long before such hours were reached. Consequently the average number of hours in use might be reduced to single figures, the rest of the time spent being serviced and prepared. Note, too, the condition of the track, typical for a locomotive depot where generations of ash and dust have compacted around the rails and sleepers.

ABOVE The quintessential Great Western branch line is represented here by '45xx' No 4552 and a short freight at Moorswater on 18 July 1960. This locations was the meeting of the Liskeard & Caradon and Liskeard & Looe lines, and also the site of a china clay works. Two engines were outstationed here, either from St Blazey or Laira, and for nearly the last forty years of their life it was this type of 'small Prairie' that was associated with the clay trains as well as passenger workings between Liskeard and Looe. The normal practice at such outstations would be to have a 'driver in charge' appointed, who would be remunerated with a small additional amount in his weekly pay packet to ensure that the depot was kept in order, rosters worked out and paperwork dealt with. Additionally there would likely be a shed man, usually working a night shift, who prepared the engines for the morning turns as well as acting as security. Notwithstanding the short train, which could hardly have been considered economic, the railway was certainly profitable from the amount of mineral traffic carried, and while china clay and indeed the engine shed (which closed in 1961) are but distant memories, there is still much rail movement as the site is now a cement distribution depot, and diesel units still traverse the passenger line from Liskeard to Looe. Out of sight to the left was a workshop and carriage shed, while water and coal were available from the tank and a small loading platform beyond.

British Railways in Unseen Colour: 1948-1962

Regardless of personal allegiance, no one can deny that the Gresley 'A4' was an impressive machine when seen from any angle. The type was aptly described in the 1954 film *Elizabethan Express*: 'Sir Nigel Gresley designed his A4 with the speed of a greyhound – the strength of a boar…' The film is well worth watching, although the 'A4' featured is not No 60003 *Andrew K. McCosh* seen here. Thirty-five of the 'A4' Class were built at Doncaster between 1935 and 1938 and were originally fitted with valancing over the top half of the driving wheels. This was removed during the war to assist maintenance. One engine, No 4469 *Sir Ralph Wedgwood*, was destroyed when it received a direct hit on York engine shed in April 1942, especially unfortunate as the engine had just been overhauled at Gateshead and was engaged on running-in turns. The names chosen for the class were varied, including individuals, empire locations and, characteristically, birds of prey; for example, No 60003 was named *Osprey* until October 1942. Instantly recognisable because of their shape, one of the class, then No 4468 *Mallard*, achieved a world record speed for steam on 3 July 1938 when 126mph was reached, a record that has never been broken.

In BR days the type were either seen in dark blue or latterly a Brunswick green, reminiscent of Great Western colours, but it suited them well. All at the peak of development at the time of their introduction, modifications to the inside big-end and the fitting of double Kylchap chimneys from 1956 onwards made an impressive machine better still, and it was not until the advent of the 'Deltic' diesels that any modern motive power was able to surpass their abilities, but even then not their top speed capabilities. Withdrawals started in December 1962, gathering pace as the years progressed until the final two went in September 1966. Due to their enduring appeal six have survived, two in North America, and all came together at the NRM, York, during 2014 for the highly successful 'Great Gathering', a scenario that we are unlikely to see repeated.

No 60003 appears here in ex-works condition following overhaul and from the white painted cab roof appears to be being prepared for a special working, probably a 'Royal' from Stamford on 17 June 1961. It had a life of just over 25 years from 12 August 1937 to 29 December 1962, one of the first five of the class to be taken out of service on the same day; none of these early withdrawals would survive into preservation. Alongside is 'A3' No 60055 *Woolwinder*, perhaps in not quite such a gleaming condition. It also has the small smoke deflectors on each side of the chimney, while others either had none or the larger German-type design from halfway up the smokebox.

Busy times at the east end of Truro. A brand-new DMU stands in the sidings, its oil tail lamp showing that it is not yet ready for its next duty. Alongside are spare passenger coaches and cattle vans, as well as the paraphernalia of a working goods yard. Alongside, a diesel shunter is busy pulling wagons towards the camera – we can tell this as the top ground signal facing the camera is 'on'. In the background is the 264-yard Carvedras Viaduct, and beyond that Truro Cattle Pens signal box with its sidings behind. On the right is the bulk of the city's cathedral. Today the main line survives, but all the sidings hereabouts have gone, with much of what was formerly railway land also redeveloped. There is also no shunting at the station, although for the moment at least some mechanical signalling survives, albeit very much on borrowed time.

Here's an even busier Norwich Thorpe, as 'Britannia' No 70007 *Coeur-de-Lion* arrives at the terminus in September 1960 with a passenger working from Liverpool Street. Very much in the changeover period from steam to diesel, examples of the more modern motive power can be seen in the station, although to be fair the steam engine was only seven years old at the time. Compare carefully this view with that of No 70003 seen earlier; No 70007 retains the handrails on the smoke deflectors, which is perhaps why the driver (it is definitely the driver as these engines were left-hand drive) is leaning from the cab to maximise his view. Something is or has also been happening on the left as there is quite a gathering of men in the 'four foot'.

Spare coaching stock also abounds – these were the days when trains were made up of various vehicles not always in the same order from one day to the next and for which purpose a 'carriage or station pilot' engine would be involved. This pilot engine would also couple up to arriving trains ready to pull back the coaches to release the arriving engine. Mechanical signalling also abounds, together with its associated point rodding and signal wires. One signal, that nearest the camera, displays a white diamond, meaning that the line passing it is track-circuited and the presence of a train stopped there will be known to the signalman.

No 70007 looks in good external condition and while it is obvious that some coal has been used what remains is substantial and also appears of good quality. Again, none of the motive power or rolling stock is in use today, all consigned to memory. No 70007 had a life of just fourteen years and, like most of the Eastern Region 'Britannia' Class, was transferred to the LMR and ended its working days at Carlisle. It would not be saved for preservation.

South now to the New Forest, much of which is heathland rather than trees, as the name might otherwise imply. Here Roy may well have been caught slightly unawares, or perhaps he was in a hurry, for this somewhat unusual image is taken looking across the main Southampton-Bournemouth main line west of Brockenhurst not far from Lymington Junction. At the latter point the old main line curved away two lines diverged; to the south-east was the short branch to Lymington, while north-west was the route to Ringwood and Wimborne, aka 'Castleman's Corkscrew'. The latter was the original line to Bournemouth and Wimborne, and was so named because it took a devious and often curving route, Castleman being a solicitor who championed the cause.

It is a Lymington train that we are observing in May 1957, an 'M7' with a three-coach 'pull-push' set, definitely in the 'push' mode with the fireman alone on the engine and the driver in the front of the first coach. Unlike what we saw earlier on the WR, on the Southern control of the engine from the coach was by compressed air, which meant that more than two vehicles could be propelled. The system worked well; indeed, as the 'M7' Class was slowly retired through age, British Railways fitted out some more modern replacements and together they would see out the end of pull-push working – of this type at least. (Electric pull-push operation was used from Waterloo to Bournemouth and Weymouth as a replacement for steam for 20-plus years after the abolition of steam in 1967.)

Today the Lymington branch survives, operated as an electric shuttle service from Brockenhurst to Lymington Town and also the Pier, for the ferry to Yarmouth on the Isle of Wight. The Ringwood/Wimborne line closed in 1964, but the present main line via Sway was electrified in 1967 and is still in operation.

Open cab 1F shunter No 41835 is clean and likely fresh from overhaul at Derby on 24 September 1961. As might be correctly assumed, this was another relic from a past age – 1892 to be precise – yet when recorded it still had a further five years of life left. Indeed, sometimes it was the older types that lasted in service the longest, as witness also the LBSCR 'Terrier' type. No 41835 was built for the Midland Railway at Vulcan Foundry, Newton-le-Willows, to the design of Samuel W. Johnson. Most of its time appears to have been spent in the north Midlands on shunting duties, where the crew would have been exposed to the rain and sleet coming off the Pennines without the benefit of any protection at the rear of the cab. The longevity of the type was solely due to a contract signed in 1866 between the Midland Railway and the Staveley Ironworks near Chesterfield, whereby the railway would provide shunting engines for 100 years, and this class was the only one suitable for the duty. BR No 41708 is the sole survivor of the 185 built; seventy-two passed to BR in 1948 and by 1961 only eleven remained. The last five were withdrawn in 1965.

LNER-design 'B1' No 61054 stands at Stratford shed on 24 April 1960. Built just into BR days in April 1948 by the North British Locomotive Co, this engine had a short life, just 16 years 2 months and 14 days to be exact when withdrawn, likely redundant as much as unserviceable. In the 1950s the 'B1' Class often worked turn and turn about with the larger 'Britannia' type on the principal Great Eastern line services, but with schedules based on the larger machines they often had to be flogged mercilessly. According to the late R. N. H. 'Dick' Hardy, who was a senior member of the Motive Power Department on the Eastern Region in the 1950s, they could also quickly become rough riders and as such certain engines were not always popular with their allocated crews – see Dick Hardy's biography of those times, *Steam in the Blood* (Ian Allan, 1971). Official records give the last date for shopping of the engine as between November 1959 and February 1960, when it was out of service for 104 days receiving a general overhaul at Stratford. By the end of September 1962, when it ceased to work, it was probably well into the 'rough' category – but then every machine, whether it be a steam engine or anything else, needs maintenance from time to time, and there were simply not the resources or the will to expend money on steam when its life was clearly coming to an end. Hence maintenance that only a few years earlier would have been carried out was curtailed, or was the cause of an engine ceasing work.

As seen here No 61054 is in reasonable external condition at least, and awaits its next duty, while lurking behind is a grimy and unidentified 'K3' 2-6-0. As steam surrendered to diesel, seventeen 'B1s' were taken into departmental stock between 1963 and 1966 for steam-heating duties. Their coupling rods, etc, were retained so they could move under their own power, but couplings were removed so they could not be used in service. Renumbered 17 to 32, the last, the former No 61315, was not taken out of service until 1968. With one exception, which made its way to Barry scrapyard, all the departmental locos were scrapped, but two of the class have been saved.

LEFT Former Swansea Harbour Trust 0-4-0ST No 1142 is seen in BR days. The SHT was an independent concern dating back to 1791, whose role (nowadays we would call it a 'mission statement') was to 'repair, enlarge and preserve the Harbour of Swansea'. This included both the widening and deepening of the entrance channel to allow for larger vessels, as well as breakwaters and a lighthouse. Subsequently the docks were enlarged, and as might be expected coal was the principal export traffic handled. As the docks expanded so did a network of railway lines within them, and the Trust acquired several steam locomotives, including this tank engine from the builder Hudswell Clarke in 1911. The GWR took over the docks in 1923 and with it several steam engines, all of the 0-4-0T type and with a short wheelbase dictated by the sharp curves that abounded. Six survived into BR days – one Barclay, three Pecketts, one Hawthorn Leslie and the Hudswell Clarke depicted here. As No 1142 it survived in service until November 1959, and is seen here at Danygraig. Records indicate that it may well have spend the last two years of its life at Shrewsbury, although what work it may have been used for there is uncertain.

RIGHT A station slumbering: this is Coltishall, the first station west from the junction at Wroxham en route to County School. The line between these two points was originally part of the East Norfolk Railway, whose main line ran 25 miles north from Norwich to Cromer and included a branch to County School. The Cromer line opened in 1874 and the branch five years later in 1879. Today the main line is still open to passengers but the branch lost its service in 1952, with through freight traffic being withdrawn in 1981 – notwithstanding a weed-killing train having traversed the route in 1983! In this undated view signalling is still present, although 'long-section' operation is clearly in use, as the stop signals in each direction are both showing 'off' (note that one is lower-quadrant and the other the more modern upper-quadrant type). Part of the route from Wroxham as far as Aylesham reopened in 1990 as the narrow-gauge Bure Valley Railway, while the main station building survives in private ownership and offers bed and breakfast accommodation. Coltishall ceased to deal with local freight from 1965, although at the time of Roy's visit coal was certainly still being handled and likely some limited general goods judging from the wagons on the left. Otherwise the rust on the rails in the sidings on the right indicates that it is clearly some time since they had anything pass over them.

Vale of Rheidol Railway No 8 *Llewelyn* is seen at Aberystwyth on 23 June 1956 soon after being repainted in green and named for the first time. (All three of the line's engines, Nos 7, 8 and 9, had previously been un-named and had carried black livery since 1948.) The history of the three engines is interesting, to say the least. Nos 7 and 8 were built new at Swindon in 1923 to replace two earlier and then ageing machines numbered 1212 and 1213. Upon completion of the new engines, the two older ones were withdrawn, ostensibly for overhaul, but No 1213 was scrapped and No 1212 repaired and returned to the line as a spare engine. Meanwhile a third totally new engine was quietly built at Swindon, No 9, and despatched to Aberystwyth masquerading as No 1213! This pleased Swindon, the narrow-gauge line, the accountants and the GWR Board, who had not been prepared to sanction three new engines even if that was what was actually needed. Consequently the railway got its new engines, and the overhauled No 1212 was not taken away for scrap until 1932.

The VofR line has been operating since 1902 and is truly one of the 'Great Little Railways of Wales'. Unlike its neighbours, which start their mountainous climbs soon after leaving their respective terminal stations, the VofR wanders through fields for some distance, causing the traveller to doubt that it will ever start to climb – but when that climb starts it really does and the sound of a steam engine working hard is a joy to behold. This is a railway well worth a visit – and another – and another.

ABOVE This is one of five standard-gauge petrol-engined service locos operated by the Western Region of British Railways after 1948 and displaying faded GWR green. (There is no brass numberplate, but there is a builder's identification plate on one end.) Used at various depots and yards such as the Hayes creosote works and the Taunton concrete works, these strange-looking machines were built by the Motor Rail Company between 1923 and 1927, with four remaining 'on the books' until 1960. The number series was 15, 23, 24, 26 and 27, with Nos 22 and 25 allocated to a pair of similar 2-foot-gauge petrol shunters supplied by the same firm in 1930. This is No 26 at Swindon on 16 June 1957. probably 'out to grass' and perhaps unlikely to work again. Of interest too are the various spares and parts lying around in what is probably the Rodbourne Lane yard: pipework for specific engines, similar platework and, beyond, spare smokebox doors and boiler rings – oh, to be able to go back and rummage today! Alongside is a 12-ton hand crane, with the folded boarding where one or two men would stand – a similar board was situated on the other side – to wind large handles that would slowly lift or lower a load through reduction gearing. The large box is a counterbalance weight.

RIGHT A pair of North British Type 2 diesel-hydraulic locos round the curve of the Western Region line from the Penzance direction soon to join the Southern route coming in from the left at Devonport Junction on 28 May 1960. There is no clue as to the working, although 'A' class discs are displayed. This was close to the time when mechanical signalling would be replaced in the Plymouth area, ceasing to operate from 26 November 1960. Mention has previously been made of how the class was used west of Plymouth, where their maximum speed of 75mph was sufficient. The locos were also employed on local work around Bristol, and could be seen on empty carriage workings between Paddington and Old Oak Common as replacements for the steam pannier tanks, including the '15xx' series of engines seen earlier. Aesthetic changes over time included the provision of split headcode boxes, while about half the class were repainted in Corporate Blue. Notwithstanding the loss of the intended survivor to scrap, in March 2014 'The Project Class 22 Society' was established with the intention of building an example of the type; details may be found at http://project22society.co.uk.

The sole surviving example of the LNER Holden-design 'B12' 4-6-0, No 61572, was photographed at Norwich on 31 May 1960 in clean black livery as befitted its celebrity status. Built in June 1928 to a design dating back to 1911, No 8572 came about due to a shortage of express steam types for use in East Anglia and the decision was made by the Chief Mechanical Engineer of the LNER, Nigel Gresley, to order ten of the type from Beyer Peacock. Variously modified over the years, particularly in relation to the inside valve gear, the design was unusual in being a large passenger engine without outside cylinders. The engine was renumbered 1572 in June 1946, British Railways adding 60,000 to the number in May 1948. All but No 61572 had been withdrawn by 1959, and this engine might have suffered a similar fate for soon after transfer to Norwich in October 1959 it was stopped with a suspected cracked cylinder. Here fortune came to the rescue in the shape of the Norwich shedmaster, Bill Harvey. He had an affection for the type and had it examined, the failure being more accurately diagnosed as simple pitting. The engine was repaired and reinstated, earning its day-to-day worth on both goods and passenger turns. Meanwhile the embryo Midland & Great Northern Joint Railway Society was raising funds, and when the time finally came for No 61572 to be withdrawn it was taken to Stratford and stored before being purchased by the society in 1963 (together with 'J15' No 65462). Restoration of the 'B12' to working order would take many years, much of the work being undertaken in Germany, and it was eventually restored to steam in 1995.

This full view of 'D16/3' 4-4-0 No 62613 was taken at March on 28 May 1960. In the right background is the coaling tower, which would hoist a full wagon of coal into the air, rotate it so that the contents fell into a hopper, then deposit the requisite amount of coal into the tender – or bunker – of an engine beneath. The obvious disadvantage was the dust, the area of any steam shed being liberally covered with fine coal dust, especially in the vicinity of the coaling stage. The other disadvantage was that during the process, and dependent upon the type being used, the coal would break up into fine pieces that was either ejected through the locomotive's fire tubes without having released any of its energy, or congeal into a mass in the firebox, restricting air flow and causing poor steaming. Here the atmosphere around the engine appears to have had a good sprinkling of fine particles of coal, with what grass there is bravely trying to establish itself in an otherwise hostile environment. Mention has previously been made of the condition of the track in the vicinity of a shed or depot, which tended to receive minimal maintenance, with reactive rather than preventative measures often being applied. As an example, look at the wooden keys in the chairs on two of the sleepers just ahead of the engine, which are only just holding the rails to gauge.

On the engine itself adornments such as the Westinghouse air pump and dual air/vacuum braking will be noted, as will the mechanical lubricator for the inside cylinders. Finally notice the painting of the front guard irons, their position on the buffer beam dictating that they are partly red before curving away below the footplate, a painting style that was unusual but was also applied to other GER engines (see the previous 'B12' image).

LEFT Metropolitan electric locomotive No 1 *John Lyon* is attached to a wooden-bodied coach at Neasden on 1 June 1957. This is probably stock for a train on the Chesham branch, which was still being worked by locomotives and separate carriages until 1961. The locomotives' withdrawal and replacement by conventional electric units coincided with a desperate situation that had arisen on the embryo Bluebell Railway. The newly preserved line was proving popular, too popular in fact, for the two former Southern coaches then in use, and the search was on for further vehicles that might be purchased at a bargain price. London Transport had six vehicles for sale at just £65 each, and the Bluebell purchased four – a fifth was saved for the London Transport Museum, while the final vehicle went for scrap. It was a good deal so far as the Bluebell was concerned, and the newly acquired coaches served the line well for many years.

Operationally such vehicles were never popular with signalmen due to the position of the door handles. One of the duties of a signalman is to observe a train that passes him for any signs of problems or distress, which includes looking at the door handles to ensure all are horizontal – in the fully closed position – otherwise it could mean that a door is not closed properly. But just look at the door handles here – the doors are closed but the handles are certainly not all in line. (Each signalman could only see the doors on one side of the train, of course, but signal boxes were not always on the same side of the line.) LNER-built stock tended to display the same trend. When its use on passenger trains was discontinued, No 1 was used for a short time as a depot shunter before being withdrawn in 1962.

OPPOSITE BOTTOM An unidentified Brush Type 2 diesel is either shunting at or leaving Whitwell & Reepham station on 20 April 1960. Although no number is visible, we can say that it is not one of the first twenty of the class as these were not fitted with rooftop indicators, as described in an earlier caption. Whitwell & Reepham was part of the Midland & Great Northern system, whose main line ran eastwards from Peterborough to the Norfolk coast, with branches north and south from Melton Constable. Whitwell & Reepham was on the section south from Melton towards Norwich (City). The station was opened in 1882, a year after the Great Eastern had opened its own, more conveniently situated facility on its line from County School to Wroxham. Notwithstanding this and the generally rural area that the M&GN traversed, the line survived until the post-war boom in private motoring resulted in closure to passengers from 28 February 1959. The same year saw most of the M&GN suffer the same fate, the first major closure by the Eastern Region of British Railways; there would be many more to come. Freight continued to be handled until May 1964, although the track remained in situ for a further twenty-one years as far as the next station south at Lenwade, as concrete products were being handled. Today the station is a preservation site with track relaid, and the owner of the station house is an enthusiastic supporter of a return of the railway, in the area of the station at least.

Despite being photographed a year after closure to passengers, all is neat and tidy with the cess free from weeds and the whole seemingly in good condition. In the background, the starting signal in the 'off' position is of the 'somersault' type, while the front of the engine is just passing over the cover of the facing point lock at the end of the loop. Notice the different levels between the running line and the headshunt on the right; the latter will have been laid on the level, so the running line clearly dips at this point, and on a fairly steep gradient.

ABOVE The first of three Southern Region views shows 'O2' No 30192, already seen earlier, at the outstation shed of Callington in May 1957. Opened around 1908, the shed here was a simple feature with corrugated iron around a timber frame supported by a dwarf brick wall. The Callington branch had originally been built as a 3ft 6in-gauge light railway, but was purchased by the Plymouth, Devonport & South Western Junction Railway in 1894 and converted to standard gauge. The new shed replaced a smaller shed on the same site that had previously been used to service the narrow-gauge engines. A space for ashes was provided outside the shed, while in later years there was also a coal stage for manual coaling. However, it was the practice for just one of the resident engines to be actually placed under cover, with the second on the same line reposing outside; the second line was used for coal wagons, as seen here. No doubt this was a local arrangement and saved the coal being transhipped twice: from the wagon to the coal stage, then into the engine bunker. For most of its life the depot was a sub-shed of Plymouth Friary, with an allocation, certainly in early years, of a pair of PD&SWJR 0-6-2 tank engines. Latterly LSWR 'O2' types also appeared, and by 1954/55 the former 0-6-2Ts were rarely seen, having been replaced by the modern Ivatt 2-6-2T type. With changing times so the depot passed to the Western Region, with control exercised from Exmouth Junction, but this was to be a short-lived arrangement as the depot closed in September 1964 and was demolished soon after.

This special working at Hayling Island on a grey 24 February 1957 was the Locomotive Club of Great Britain's 'Southern Counties Tour', which, like many rail tours before and since, involved a varied selection of motive power over a variety of routes. Who, for example, would ordinarily leave London Marylebone for Hayling Island? Well, this train did (with a few other destinations en route!), starting with double-headed 'N5' 0-6-2T locos Nos 69257 and 69319 from Marylebone to Kew East Junction, travelling via Wembley Stadium. Then the ER engines came off and were replaced by 'H2' 'Atlantic' No 32424 *Beachy Head*, which took the train on to the next changeover point at Horsted Keynes via Clapham Junction, Factory Junction, Nunhead, Lewisham, Sanderstead and East Grinstead. While today we rightly associate Horsted Keynes with the Bluebell Railway, at the time it was still a BR operation (in its 'transient' days having been forced to reopen due to the closure not complying with the original Act of Parliament for the railway), and it was here that a 'C2X' 0-6-0 took over for the run to Brighton via Sheffield Park and Lewes. The 'C2X' was then turned and continued with the train the short distance to Preston Park, where 'Standard 4' tank No 80152 was attached for the run along the coast west through Worthing and Chichester to Havant. There No 80152 was temporarily detached and two of the diminutive 'Terriers' came on, one at each end of the six-coach formation, and these 'topped and tailed' the train over the Hayling Island branch before returning to Havant. No 80152 took over once more for the short journey to the terminus at Portsmouth Harbour. Finally 'Schools' No 30929 *Malvern* was coupled to the other end for the final leg to London (Waterloo) via Guildford. As well might be said, 'A grand day out'!

The train is seen here at the terminus at Hayling Island with the signal cleared ready for its return. The small size of No 32650 is apparent compared with the standard coaching stock; the 'Terriers' were the only engines permitted to operate the branch due to weight restrictions over the wooden Langstone Bridge. Two or three coaches was also the standard load for branch trains, hence the need for an engine at each end, although in any event it is unlikely that there would have been enough room to run round this length of train at Hayling.

Sister engine to No 30585 seen earlier, Beattie-designed 'Well Tank' No 30586 is seen shunting the yard at Wadebridge on 16 June 1960. The term 'Well Tank' comes from the fact that most of the engine's water was carried in a tank mounted between the frames, compared with other tank engines where it was variously in side, pannier or saddle tanks. (Some tender locomotives on the GWR had an additional well-tank between the frames.) The 'Well Tank' arrangement could be said to have given the engine greater stability, although the down side was the limited space available and the difficulty in keeping the tank watertight. Even so, the three engines survived in service for close on ninety years in this form, although they were never really all that far from a water supply.

As seen here all appears well, the engine is clean, the yard well stocked and the location still open to both passengers and freight. But things were to change all too soon. First, No 30586 and her two sisters were withdrawn at the end of 1962. Three years later, on 31 December 1965, passenger services were withdrawn, leaving only freight traffic, which lingered on until 1978. Today the Bodmin & Wenford heritage line is reaching out towards Wadebridge, although an earlier attempt to reintroduce china clay trains from Wenford Bridge, which would have reduced the amount of road traffic in the area, was defeated by local residents. No 30586 was the unlucky one among the trio of engines that had such a long life, as it was not saved and was destined to be scrapped.

LEFT One of the earlier images from the collection is this view of LNER No 1671 *Royal Sovereign* at Bishopsgate, just outside Liverpool Street, in August 1947, resplendent in LNER Apple Green with that railway's teak-liveried coaching stock to match. This 'B17/2' 4-6-0 was built by Messrs Robert Stephenson & Hawthorn Ltd in June 1937, but was later converted to a 'B2' type in August 1945 and subsequently served British Railways for ten years before being withdrawn in May 1958. Most if not all of its BR days were spent based at Cambridge, although there were short spells working away, for example when it underwent repairs at Darlington and obviously travelled there and back, as well as probably working running-in turns in the area. A total of seventy-three of the class were built and variously named after country residencies or football clubs – why the variation, and any possible connection between the namings, is not reported. The class was originally intended to take over work on the weight-restricted Great Eastern lines where the 'B12s' were being stretched. Built as three-cylinder engines, which would reduce the 'hammer-blow' effect on the track compared with a two-cylinder machine, the weight limitations also determined that the final drive had to be split, so the inside cylinder drove the centre coupled axle. Withdrawals started in 1952 and the last of the type was scrapped in 1960. None of the originals have been preserved, although a group has been formed with the aim of a 'new-build' project to replicate two engines of the design.

THE ARCHIVE

LEFT This view across part of the expanse of 'Top Shed' at King's Cross has Stratford-based 'B1' No 61277 prominent. The depot itself consisted of no fewer than twenty-five roads and was sited on the north side of the Regents Canal. While we may normally associate the depot with the likes of the 'A4', 'A3', 'A2', 'A1' and 'V2' types, it must not be forgotten that there were numerous other locomotive classes allocated for differing purposes; indeed, in 1948, of an allocation of 181 steam engines, 119 were what might be considered the 'less glamorous' type. As such they perhaps did not always receive attention from the cleaners on a regular basis, as indeed is seen here with the various tender and tank engines on view. No 61277, however, is the exception, and the fact that it is clean and also away from its home depot may well indicate some form of special working. On the right, 'J39' 0-6-0 No 64805 has the chalked letters 'OK' on the smokebox, indicating a recent repair; notice how its determined use as primarily a freight engine is confirmed by the three-link rather than screw coupling, and also the lack of any steam heat facility. The track immediately ahead of its neighbour, 'N7' 0-6-2T No 69654, is also worthy of a glance, displaying a pronounced dip at the fishplate.

ABOVE Back to the South West, this is Callington again, and a view of the train shed; as with the locomotive depot, it comprises corrugated sheeting over a timber frame. This was the terminus of the original branch from Bere Alston, but it was cut back to Gunnislake in November 1966. Bus competition was the principal reason for closure, the road able to provide a direct service to Plymouth over reasonable roads while the railway involved a change of train – and direction – at Bere Alston. Ironically it was the reverse at Gunnislake, where the roads were poor and the railway was the preferred means of transport. In this view, possibly also taken in May 1957, two-coach 'pull-push' set No 363 is sheltered (to an extent) from the elements while it awaits its next duty. The smoke-blackened edge to the train shed is also immediately obvious. Coach set No 363 dated back to LSWR days and was known as 'gate stock', as passenger access was via metal gates – unfortunately hidden by the pillars of the train shed; it was one of three similar sets allocated to services on the branch. On the platform is the usual paraphernalia associated with the railway of the period – fire buckets, of course, but also luggage barrows and a ladder.

This is the delightfully rural location of Penmaenpool (between Barmouth and Bala Junction) and its locomotive shed. The building beyond was a domestic house, although it is not known if it was in fact a railway property – we wonder if the occupants ever worried about an engine not stopping as it entered the shed… Between the two was a small office, while other facilities included the coaling stage made of old sleepers and a water tower – just visible on the left. It must have been unusual to say the least to have an engine shed with grass around at least two sides. The shed came about as this was close to the end of the Cambrian line, beyond which it became the GWR route from Bala. When the Great Western absorbed the Cambrian in 1923 one might have expected the depot to close, but in fact it remained in use until as late as January 1965 – the date the line also closed. At the end of 1947 the allocation was just a single 0-4-2T, but here a '58xx' 0-4-2 (the non-auto-fitted version of the '14xx' Class) and '2251' No 2234 are both present. Notwithstanding its small size it was not unusual to see a '43xx' 2-6-0 here on occasions as well.

Despite having an apparent gloomy interior, electric lighting is at least provided outside, so may well have been used inside as well. No doors are fitted, although there appear to be the remains of hinges on the right, indicating that this may not always have been the case – or perhaps something did not stop! Notice too the 'limited clearance' sign (the red and white chequerboard) on the centre pillar; this was to warn staff that it was not safe to attempt to walk between the pillar and an engine on either side, which might move. The shed measured just 60 feet by 30 feet and was originally a sub-depot of Croes Newydd. This changed when it came under Brecon, and finally in its last days it was a sub-depot of Birkenhead. Looking north towards Bala the two stop signals are both worked from Penmaenpool, and the control wires for each can be seen running alongside the track on the right. Both signals are GWR 4-foot wooden arms on a wooden post. Just beyond this by the trackside is a trespass notice.

'Austerity' 2-8-0 No 90609 passes Black Carr Sidings East, on the outskirts of Doncaster, with a train of empties for Rossington Colliery. The colliery dated from 1912-15 and was operated by British Coal until the early 1990s. Closed – temporarily – between 1993 and 1994, it reopened and was active, albeit on an ever-reducing scale, until 2007, one of the last of the former South Yorkshire pits. Following closure it was moribund for five years (the buildings were demolished in 2007) until a coal reclamation project was started in 2012 on the former pit spoil tip. Subsequently in 2015 a £100 million redevelopment started involving 1,200 houses, a school and even a hotel. When in use, coal output from the colliery was of course crucial, but equally important was a steady flow of empty wagons ready for refilling. In earlier years these wagons might have been owned by the colliery, a coal factor, or even a coal merchant, but as years passed so the older low-capacity, short-wheelbase wooden-bodied wagons gave way to the all-steel mineral type that likely forms the train behind the engine tender. (Collieries that survived to the end were sending their products away in 100-ton monster vehicles.) No 90609 was one of the 200 engines of the 2-8-0 type purchased by the LNER in 1946, originally grouped as Class 'Q7' and numbered 63000 to 63199 before all were renumbered in the 90xxx series. It survived in service until the end of October 1963, towards the end working from Hull (Dairycoates) shed.

ABOVE This was the view of the footplate crew from the cab of one of the Adams 4-4-2T engines 'somewhere' on the Lyme Regis branch on 14 July 1960. From numerous images seen of the workings on this branch, the locomotives always seemed to face towards Lyme Regis, so on that basis we shall assume that this was indeed travelling away from Axminster. The line was 6½ miles long and traversed two counties, starting at Axminster in Devon and terminating at Lyme Regis in Dorset. There was one intermediate station at Combpyne where a Camping Coach was often stabled during the summer season.

There was just one major structural feature south of the latter station, Cannington Viaduct. This structure was 203 yards long with eight arches and a maximum height of 92 feet. Opened in 1903, it was certainly one of the earlier mass concrete structures with materials being brought by sea to the harbour at Lyme, then transported to the site via a 1,000-foot cableway. During construction the west abutment and adjacent pier slipped, necessitating extra stabilising of this pier and two of the arches. Although the railway closed at the end of November 1965, the viaduct remains and is now Grade II listed.

Apart from its famed use of veteran locomotives working services for most of its life, the Lyme Regis branch had one other claim to fame at the junction with the main line at Axminster. Here the branch had a flyover across the main line so as not to disrupt main-line traffic. This was the most westerly of all the flyovers on the South Western main line, the next closest example being at Battledown, 93 miles further east. (In between there was a 'fly-under' for traffic from Amesbury heading west at Amesbury Junction.)

TOP RIGHT A return to Newton Abbot now, with 'large Prairie' No 5158 waiting outside the shed in the mid-April sunshine of 1956. The two other engines behind can be identified by type if not by number or name, being a '14xx' 0-4-2T and a '68xx' 'Grange' 4-6-0. What a wonderful heap of coal on the left as well! This was the shed's emergency supply – most depots had such a facility – and was carefully built up so that if supplies were interrupted normal working might continue, for a time at least. The whole was constructed with the same skills as a countryman might use in making a dry-stone wall, with the sides deliberately sloped to prevent collapse. Coal could 'go off' if not used, so such stacks were regularly taken down and rebuilt usually during the summer months.

No 5158, this was one of several variants of the 2-6-2T wheel arrangement, which included the '31xx', '3150', '41xx'/'51xx', '61xx' and '81xx' classes. The differences between the types involved wheel diameter, cylinder capacity, boiler pressure and, in consequence, weight – and thus of course use. They were all powerful and useful machines, and No 5158 was one of several based here whose duties would include local passenger and freight as well as pilot duties over the South Devon banks between Newton Abbot and Plymouth. (The South Devon banks always saw pilot assisting, never banking.) No 5158 was built at Swindon in 1930 and in 1934 is shown as based at Bristol Bath Road. At some stage it moved to St Blazey, but by 1948 was at Newton Abbot, where it would remain for the rest of its working life. It was withdrawn from that shed in April 1961 and scrapped three months later.

BOTTOM RIGHT Another shed view, this time eastwards at Exeter St David's, where two variations of the 'pannier' type repose in the sunshine. On the left is '84xx' No 8456, with another similar engine behind, while to the right is '57xx' No 9765 and, behind it, a '22xx' 0-6-0. Exeter to Newton Abbot is something like 18 rail miles, yet it was not uncommon to have major steam depots in such close proximity. One of the reasons for this was historic, while another depended on the lines radiating from the specific location, the topography of these routes and in consequence the motive power needs of the area. Indeed, on the main line between London Paddington and Penzance in the period from, say, 1930 onwards the there were no fewer than eleven main steam sheds (excluding stabling points and local depots), at Old Oak Common, Southall, Slough, Reading, Westbury, Taunton, Exeter St David's, Newton Abbot, Plymouth, Truro and Penzance. Exeter was a four-road covered depot and was similar to that at Weymouth. There was also a lifting/repair shop, turntable, coaling and water facilities and the usual offices. It was located opposite the up relief platform so, assuming the latter was not occupied, a good view of the depot could be had from that vantage point. (But there was invariably something just blocking what one was perhaps most interested in seeing!)

No 8456 was one of the final variants of the inside-cylinder pannier tank, having the water tanks stopping short of the smokebox, and was a design introduced from 1947 onwards. This one was built by the Yorkshire Engine Company to a Swindon design in 1950 and spend the first eight years of its life in the West Country, nearly all at Exeter, before moving to Southall at the end of November 1958. Almost five years to the day later it was withdrawn from there. No 9765 dated from 1935, yet shared many features in common with its younger sister – cylinder size, wheel diameter, boiler pressure, etc. It came to Exeter in 1953 and ended its days on New Year's Eve 1961, making two final trips, first to Swindon, then towed to Cashmore at Newport where it was broken up in April 1962.

British Railways in Unseen Colour: 1948-1962

This LNER Class 'J15' 0-6-0, formerly Great Eastern 'Y14', is seen as BR No 65469 at Norwich on 31 May 1960. The design dated back to July 1883 when the first of what would be 259 engines in twenty-seven different batches was constructed. No 571, as it then was, was erected at Stratford Works in May 1912. Although small by modern-day standards, this was a useful and long-lived type, and held one specific record that will likely never be beaten today. This was for the time it took to built one of the class in 1913, when No 930 was assembled at Stratford (albeit from pre-prepared components) in the remarkable time of 9 hours and 45 minutes, totally beating the previous British record of 25 hours 30 minutes for a Webb 0-6-0 built at Crewe. After being steamed and photographed, No 930 went straight into revenue service, not returning to Stratford for servicing until some 5,000 miles later. Although built primarily for freight, these engines were also used on excursion and troop trains until train weights and speeds increased, after which they were confined to light branch-line duties. During the First World War forty-three were loaned for service in France and Belgium, and all eventually returned except one, No 513, which was so badly worn out that it was withdrawn. A further sixteen went in 1922. Subsequently, the engines were slowly laid aside, but just under half of those built, 127 of the 259, passed to BR in 1948. No 65469 was one of the final few to survive and was withdrawn from March week-ended 23 June 1962. One of the class, No 65462, was purchased for preservation.

This final look at the Isle of Wight shows No W16 *Ventnor*, appropriately, on an evening Ventnor to Ryde stopping service running along the pier at Ryde towards its final stop at Ryde Pier Head station on 24 May 1960. In the background is Ryde Esplanade station and the town itself. Running alongside the railway is the Ryde Pier tramway, which linked the Pier and Esplanade stations and was of considerable benefit for those who were unwilling or unable to walk the 745 yards to the town – notice the walkway just visible on the right. The tramway was operational from 1864 to 1969. Upon arrival at Pier Head, No 16 (the 'W' identification appeared in paperwork but was not displayed on the cabside) will first disgorge its passengers, then run round ready for its return.

As elsewhere on the Southern Region, the discs, or lights at night, were used to primarily indicate the route of the service rather than the type of train. The single disc seen also referring to a Newport to Freshwater service, but as those trains never went anywhere near Ryde (and indeed the Freshwater line had been closed for several years when this photograph was taken) there was never likely to be any confusion. Another feature of the IoW locos was that at the front the loco number was painted on the buffer beam and smokebox numberplates were not fitted. The stock of this six-coach working is mainly in SR green, although there is one throwback to early BR days in the form of the all-red coach; this was either one of the last to have received this livery or it is an indication of just how long some vehicles might have gone between repaints. No W16 was built at Nine Elms in June 1892 and transferred to the island in 1936. It was withdrawn with the end of steam services at the end of 1966.

LEFT Sunshine and shadows: a London Transport (Metropolitan Line) train working an eastbound Aldgate service approaches Liverpool Street on 22 May 1960. The train is in the then standard all-over red livery that we associate with the Underground, and is formed of CO/CP stock. Alongside, in the dead-end siding, is the now-preserved electric locomotive No 12 *Sarah Siddons*, although at that time was still in revenue-earning service. In the foreground is paraphernalia associated with this intensively used network, including the live and return electric rails, power points and cabling – small wonder that the shine on the top of the rails of so many Underground lines never fades. The Underground units seen were first introduced in 1937 and were in regular use until 1981. Slightly unusual in the lower left of the photograph is the way the conductor rail continues across what might otherwise appear to be a board crossing. The conductor rails all have their ends tapered down to allow ease of contact with the pick-up shoes.

RIGHT Another Locomotive Club of Great Britain tour that was at least photographed by Roy, if not travelled on by him, was the London Branch's 'Poplar & Edgware' trip of Saturday 5 May 1956. This was an afternoon event starting from Broad Street at 2 o'clock with No 58859 running via Dalston Junction to Poplar Central and Poplar Dock. There another engine, No 47484, took over heading for East Ham, Stratford and Canonbury. From Canonbury it was north to the terminus at Alexandra Palace and thence back to Canonbury, but this time via Edgware. Finally at Canonbury No 58859 took over once more for the return to Broad Street, where the scheduled arrival time was 7.05pm – all this for just 7s 6d in 3rd Class. Here we see No 58859, a former North London Railway tank, at Poplar in sparkling condition and with an equally clean ex-LMS vehicle behind. The 0-6-0T is only fitted with a three-link coupling, so we can be certain that it was attached to the train using the coach's own screw variant. The location of the image is not confirmed; Roy refers to it as 'Millwall', but the itinerary does not record this as having been visited, so perhaps more likely it is Millwall Junction station.

This panoramic view of Inverness features a southbound service for Perth and beyond leaving behind a pair of 'Black 5s'. Dominating the scene is the monstrous coaling plant, perhaps of a different design from that seen at March earlier but performing the same function; a number of coal wagons may be seen nearby. Access for the operator was via the flights of steps, and once inside he would at least be protected from the worst that the Inverness Firth might throw at him, but is to be guaranteed that there would be little redress from the all-pervading coal dust that would swirl around every time either the contents of a wagon were tipped into the hopper or a similar load was deposited into a waiting engine 30 feet below. Aside from the two train engines, which are not identifiable, a third member of the same class, believed to be No 44925, stands nearby, while one engine that can be exactly determined is 0-4-4T No 55160, engaged in shunting wagons in front of the coal stage. At least one other steam engine is active in the carriage sidings in the background. Inverness station is a terminus and was for many years the location of the Lochgorm works of the original owning company, the Highland Railway. From the station routes spread out not only to Perth but also to Elgin and Dingwall. A curve allowed through working between the last two named and thus provided what was one side of a triangle at the station.

ABOVE In this unusual view of the west end of Liskeard station, a DMU is departing, probably all stations to Penzance. Despite the modern (for the period) motive power, the use of an oil tail lamp persists, and indeed would do so until the early/mid-1960s. The view is taken from the road bridge that bisected the location; we are looking at the down (westbound) platform with the up platform staggered slightly due to yard access and starting just behind the camera. There are numerous features of note, including the Western Region's standard painting scheme of 'chocolate and cream' that had superseded the 'dark and light stone' used by the GWR. One modern touch is the '6 car stop' sign on the left-hand lamp post. Lower-quadrant signals abound – of course. The down starting signal is on a bracket to give the driver the maximum view of it on the approach due to the curved track and overbridge. Notice too that the advance starting signal is also 'off', and is placed on the right-hand side of the line, again to maximise visibility – GWR locomotive designs were always driven from the right. In the yard there is the usual motley collection of vehicles, but more interesting has to be the goods shed itself, dating back to broad gauge days. The main line drops sharply away from the platform towards the next station west at Doublebois, emphasised by the difference in levels between the running lines and the yard. One particular fact about the station is that in 2018 Liskeard has the dubious distinction of being the nearest place to London on the former Great Western main line where semaphore signals could still be seen – 237 miles from the terminus at Paddington.

OPPOSITE TOP A double-headed train (with LNER and LMS locos?) leaves Kyle of Lochalsh for Dingwall and beyond. Officially the Dingwall & Skye Railway, this 63-mile line justifiably ranks as one of the most scenic railways in Britain, if not elsewhere, and has been in existence as a complete railway since November 1897. It was intended as one of the means of transporting goods to the Isle of Skye via a ferry from Kyle, but there was also competition for this traffic via the West Highland line to Mallaig, the latter also more easy to access from the south. The whole D&S route was costly to both build and to operate; indeed, the final 10 miles from Strome Ferry through to Kyle was built almost exclusively either through rock cuttings or on embankments and at the time was the most expensive railway per mile ever built in Britain. Somehow it survived the cuts of the 1960s, based mostly on social need, and it was that ability to serve isolated rural communities with no proper road access that saved it from closure. Closure was again considered a decade later, but its future now is more secure, with regular services as well as excursion traffic.

One interesting feature of the line, which was a carry-over from years past, was the practice of passengers being able to travel in the brake vans of freight trains. This was permitted provided that they had paid a fare and recognised that it was at their own risk. This practice continued until the demise of freight trains over the line in the 1970s, and had originally come about from the need for perhaps a doctor or vet to be able to reach an isolated house or farm with no easy road access after the passenger trains had ceased running for the day or there was no service scheduled for some time. (How the said worthy might return was not mentioned!)

RIGHT Ipswich station is seen on 14 May 1959 from the fireman's side of a 'Britannia' locomotive. From Ipswich there were once routes to London via Colchester, to Cambridge, Felixstowe, Beccles and, as the blind on the DMU states, Yarmouth – a long 60-plus miles in a rattling DMU that stopped at every station. That said, there was at least a view through the driver's front windows, provided that he did not pull down the blinds behind his seat! The set in the adjacent platform is a Cravens 'twin', built by that company at its Darnall (Sheffield) works and produced both in two- and three-car formations, as well as three single-unit motor parcels vans. This was one of the early DMU designs introduced from 1956 onwards, and originally had 150hp AEC diesel engines fitted; the units also had a body profile identical to that of the latest Mk 1 passenger coaches. The set is in the smart early livery selected for DMUs that suited them so well, namely overall green with white lines at the centre and cantrail and 'speed whiskers' at the front. The latter were intended to give men working on the track some warning of the unit's approach – later superseded, of course, by yellow panels, then full yellow ends. In later years the centre headcode panels were removed. The units were active until the early 1980s, the last being taken out of service in 1988.

127

An unidentified 'D8xx' member of the 'Warship' Class heads 'The Royal Duchy' express some time in July 1961. This train was introduced by the Western Region of British Railways in 1957, running each way between London Paddington and, as the name might well suggest, Penzance in Cornwall. The practice of naming trains was certainly not new and has fallen in and out of favour over the years. BR gave names to several other services around this time, including the 'Caledonian' (Glasgow Central-London Euston), 'Cathedrals Express' (London Paddington-Oxford-Hereford), 'Fair Maid' (London King's Cross-Perth), 'Mayflower' (Kingswear and Plymouth to London Paddington), and 'Waverley' (Edinburgh Waverley-Carlisle Citadel-Leeds City-London St Pancras).

The 'D8xx' 'Warships' were split into two types: those numbered D800-32 and D866-70 were built by BR at Swindon, while Nos D833-65 came from the North British Locomotive Company. Both were diesel-hydraulic machines but differed in both engine and transmission types. The class was based on a German design, scaled down for the British loading gauge, and hydraulic rather than electric transmission was chosen for two reasons: the torque available at slow speeds over steep gradients, especially those of the South Devon banks that would be a regular feature of their working, and also the WR's poor experience of the electric transmission fitted to the gas-turbine electric No 18000 when this was working on the WR from 1951 onwards. To be fair, at the time it was not realised how important it was to keep the electrical transmission parts clean; failure to do so contributed to the high levels of failure on No 18000. The engine seen here is attached to a short rake of six BR Mk1 vehicles, certainly not the full formation of the train; the location is not given, but the picture was most probably taken somewhere west of Plymouth, where the formation would have been split. Carriage roofboards are also carried, while the locomotive has a steam-engine-style train nameboard.

RIGHT Fresh from overhaul at Crewe, Fairburn 2-6-4T No 42674 is seen outside the works on 19 March 1960. The LMS/LMR had more than 570 of these useful 2-6-4 tank engines, the first dating back to 1927. Over the years the design was modified and that seen represents the final development, built between 1945 and 1951, this one emerging from Derby in April 1945. It entered service as No 2674, the '4' prefix being added soon after nationalisation. Most of its working life appears to have spent at Stoke, that is until it was declared redundant and withdrawn in November 1962 and disposed of back at Derby in January 1963.

After nationalisation forty-one were built by the Southern Region at Brighton, thirty-four of them remaining with the Southern to fill a desperate need for a large – but stable – passenger tank engine. The remaining seven were sent to the North Eastern Region between the spring of 1952 and the end of 1954. The Southern examples stayed with that region until 1959 when they were moved to their spiritual home on the LMR in exchange for an equivalent number of BR Class 4 2-6-4Ts, the two designs having much in common. The class was intact until 1961, when withdrawals commenced and accelerated through to 1963, when fifty-seven were condemned. The last went in 1967, although two have been preserved, both Brighton engines, and are currently on the heritage Lakeside & Haverthwaite Railway.

LEFT Here is a second view of one of the Wolverton Carriage Department shunters, complete with brass plate, but date and location unknown. While aesthetically the design shows its age, it certainly appears to be in reasonable external condition and is likely well cared for. A BR crest may also be noted on the saddle tank. At some stage in its life an enclosed cab has been fitted, and some form of cab protection has been achieved in the form of a curtain/storm sheet. Atop the firebox is a Ramsbottom-style safety valve, and the water tank filler on the tank is open. Finally notice the spokes on the wheels (compare with the next locomotive portrait), a much heavier and flatter design than was commonplace in later years.

ABOVE Another locomotive view shows this time an LNER 'J35' 0-6-0 to the design of W. P. 'Willie' Reid, seventy-six of which were built by the North British Railway in batches between 1906 and 1913. They came either from the NBR's own workshop at Cowlairs or from the North British Locomotive Co. As built they were not fitted with superheaters and as such were classified as 'saturated' engines, although retro-fitting took place across the whole class between 1923 and 1942. Originally given long-distance goods duties, they were ousted from that type of work from 1914 onwards and instead found a use on coal trains as well as local pick-up goods traffic. Despite being built as freight engines, they could also be found on main-line passenger work in the summer months. (Norman McKillop gives a vivid description of working the 'J35' and other NBR classes out of Edinburgh Haymarket shed in his book *Engineman Elite*.) The class was intact until 1946 and all but six passed to BR in 1948, still working mainly over the routes they had been developed for. Aside from the six early casualties the remainder were still at work until 1958, but inroads were then rapidly made and the type was extinct by December 1962. None survived into preservation.

Seen here is BR No 64487 at the shed at Alloa on 21 April 1957. Built in September 1909 by the North British Locomotive Co at its Queen's Park Works in Glasgow, it had a service life of just over fifty years; it was placed into store on 30 May 1959 but never reprieved and was withdrawn in April 1960. Typical of the NBR designs were the single rounded cabside window and the semi-circular curved handrail midway up the smokebox door, which according to some gave the engine a 'sad' appearance when viewed from the front. The engine behind is not identified.

RIGHT This is the view from the coal stage at Laira (Plymouth) looking back towards Laira Junction, where we saw No 6873 *Caradoc Grange* earlier. The carriage sidings mentioned then are now visible on the left, with an auto-coach just visible. Creeping into view on the extreme left is a Collett corridor vehicle in 'blood and custard' livery. Roy's picture is looking east, with the incline running up to the coal stage on the right – notice the catchpoint at the bottom of the gradient, something that was always provided at the foot of an incline leading to a coal stage in the event of a wagon breaking free at the top.

The GWR never had any coal hoppers at any of its sheds like those we have seen at March and Inverness. This was because its engines used Welsh coal, which was soft and in consequence more likely to break and crumble if discharged from a great height. Coaling was thus done by hand at Laira and elsewhere on the Western, the coal being shovelled out of the arriving coal wagons into tubs, which were then wheeled across a metal floor to be tipped into the waiting tender/bunker a few feet below. Full coal wagons bringing extra supplies for hungry engines are to be seen on the right, and possibly also those on the extreme left. Coal would have been handled at Plymouth for domestic purposes – almost without exception every house seen in the background has a chimney – although by this period coal as a fuel was no longer needed for the naval fleet at nearby Devonport.

The depot is engaged in a 'shunt' of sorts, with at least five engines that all appear to be out of or at best in light steam being moved by the depot shunter at the far end. The combined weight of these five with their laden tenders would exceed 500 tons, so a fair amount of effort would be required, added to which would be the resistance and compression from the cylinders – the shunt crew would have checked to see that the cylinder cocks were open on all the engines being moved.

Overall this view is so typical of the hundreds of steam sheds around the country: a smoky atmosphere that would cling close to the ground especially during an anti-cyclone when the air was still or slow-moving. Today we would refer to it as urban pollution, which was what it was of course, made worse not just by weather conditions but when a large number of engines were being prepared for duty at any one time. Hanging clean washing out to dry did not guarantee that it would come in clean later. None of the engines are particularly clean; indeed, as time went by the

recruiting of engine cleaners, the first step on the ladder to a career on the footplate, was becoming increasingly difficult, and this was another feature that hastened the demise of the steam engine. Why work all hours for little pay in poor conditions when a clean job might be had in a factory, paying considerably more than British Railways could offer?

Some of the signals are interesting: two with 'ringed' arms indicate that they apply to sidings. These signals also carry what were officially 'route indicator' signals, colloquially known as 'cash registers', as any one of several route indicators could be raised to apply to each arm. That on the left, for example, could indicate that the signal had been cleared for the Up Goods, Up Loop, Spur, or Down Goods – respectively levers 4, 21, 25 or 27 in the 116-lever Laira Junction signal box just seen in the background before the overbridge. When the appropriate signal lever was pulled the specified route would show up as a stencilled display against a white background, the driver thus knowing where he was bound. The 'cash register' term derived from what we now refer to as an old-fashioned shop till, where the amount of the transaction would appear as separate tabs in a window.

Notice that between the rails ahead of the right-hand signal is a ramp. This is an ATC test ramp, and one was placed on the depot exit line at every shed. Its purpose was to test the operation of the ATC (Automatic Train Control) system fitted to ex-GWR engines; if a driver passed a distant signal at danger a warning would sound and the brakes would be applied automatically unless the driver made a conscious decision to acknowledge and cancel the warning. Finally it is worth mentioning that the tenders of all the engines seen are full, the practice being to service an engine upon its arrival on shed so it could later be quickly made ready for its next duty.

ABOVE In May 1960 Roy recorded this view of an auto-working coming off the Royal Albert Bridge and passing the signal box of the same name heading east towards Plymouth. The locomotive, the ubiquitous auto-fitted pannier tank, is sandwiched between vehicles two and three. Alongside, the first signs of the new road bridge are also rising; this will eventually run parallel with the railway across the Tamar.

Royal Albert Bridge signal box contained twenty-five levers and for decades worked with Saltash signal box either by Electric Train Staff or Electric Train Token over the single line across the bridge. For the last portion of its life, full track circuiting was provided across the bridge and Acceptance Lever working replaced the physical token. In this view notice that the ATC ramp on the down line is beyond the signal post on the right – always the case when a stop and distant arm were on the same post. One interesting quirk about the bridge was that during the Second World War wooden decking was laid between and on either side of the rails to allow military vehicles to cross between Devon and Cornwall if necessary. To safeguard this operation a human pilotman would remove a token from the signal box at whichever end the vehicle (or convoy) was starting, and ride with the vehicle, or the last one of the convoy, crossing the bridge. The first recorded such movement involved the allocated pilotman riding across on top of a Bren gun carrier, reported as a most uncomfortable experience! (Source: *Mechanical Signalling in Plymouth*, Larry Crosier, published by the Signalling Record Society.)

OPPOSITE BOTTOM Against the backdrop of York Minster, this is a view of the North Eastern Region of British Railways headquarters in September 1955, with the City walls immediately opposite. Just below the level of the walls the roofs of several rail vehicles are also visible. It was here that Roy worked during the final years of his railway career. The administration of the various railway companies is often something that is ignored by enthusiasts and historians, yet it required a veritable army of clerks to operate, record and regulate the administration of the system, a business that was as diverse as anything that could be imagined, dealing not just with locomotives, carriages, wagons, road vehicles, horses, and people – passengers, business customers and staff through to controllers, inspectors, signalmen, station masters, foremen, porters, shunters, gatekeepers, drivers, firemen, fitters, and all the rest; all records were written in full and if every grade and role was included the entries would cover several pages. Aside from staff and vehicle records, there would be financial and traffic records, details of tickets and revenue, stores from scaffolding to sheep dogs – yes, the railway had some sheep dogs on the payroll to round up sheep that might stray onto the line, especially in rural Scotland and the like, not dissimilar to today when on occasions a falconer is brought in to stations to discourage the local pigeon population.

THE ARCHIVE

LEFT Away from the West Country, this is Takeley, near Bishops Stortford in Essex, a particular favourite of the present writer. Originally part of the independent Bishops Stortford, Dunmow & Braintree Railway, the route and the station here opened on 22 February 1869, with the company absorbed into the Great Eastern Railway on the same day. Passenger services lasted until March 1952, while freight continued to be handled until August 1961. Alongside the platform had originally been a loop siding with a small goods yard at the east end, out of sight here. There was also a wooden signal box on the south side of the line, again behind the photographer. Notwithstanding the loss of regular passenger facilities, August Bank Holiday excursions used the railway until 1964. In its final years goods were no longer handled and the signalling was removed, although the empty signal box stood sentinel to what had gone before, and it was just a former stopping place on the freight line serving a factory at Braintree. In this scene regular passengers will not have graced the platforms for many years, although the porter-in-charge is still tending the station gardens. On the platform edge the wartime alternate black/white painted lines to assist passengers during the blackout can also still be seen. In recent years much of the trackbed has been converted to a walking and cycle route, and there are calls for the track to be relaid to serve increasing community demand. Takeley station itself is also now a community café.

The first of the Swindon-built D8xx series of 'Warship' Class diesel-hydraulics, and doyen of the type, was No D800 *Sir Brian Robertson*, introduced in 1958 and named after the then chairman of the British Transport Commission. There were two 'Warship' Class diesel types operating on the Western Region at the time, physically and mechanically different although both had hydraulic transmission. As was recounted earlier, this was the preferred design, having also the advantage of a far better power-to-weight ratio: 2,000hp and 78 tons against the 2,000hp and 117 tons of the D6xx series. Later variants of the D8xx class would be better still, being rated at 2,200hp.

No D800, seen here at the east end of Par station in Cornwall heading towards Plymouth and London, is clearly new in service, but was destined to have a life of just ten years. It is receiving some attention from admirers on the bridge, while two men appear somewhat underawed in the rear cab. Likely they are observers, engineers or technicians rather than passengers, as it was certainly the practice for one or more to be carried on these locomotives when they were first in passenger service and whose role was to fix any defect that occurred en route. Indeed, in a book of driver's reminiscences from years ago, when the author was recounting the early days of diesel traction, the comment was made that when the signal to go was given and the driver gingerly opened the power controller there was no guarantee that movement would take place, but instead a series of flashes or a sudden display of fault lights. A similarly cautious approach, with the assurance of a travelling fitter, was adopted during the time of the 'Blue Pullman' sets and early days of the HSTs. In reality, as experience was gained, so the D8xx series settled down well into traffic. If they had an Achilles' heel it was, as with all the early diesel locomotives, the oil-fired boiler used for train heating; this had a habit of being temperamental and more than one second-man, as the fireman's role had now become, was treated to singed eyebrows on a regular basis.

The Archive

The former GWR station at Launceston was once the terminus of trains on the GWR line from Plymouth. Opened in 1865, the station was joined by the LSWR route from Halwill Junction in 1886, and for almost the next seventy years the two companies operated side by side, from 1916 sharing a common signal box containing two frames, one for each railway. Another aspect of shared operation took place some years later when the former LSWR loco facilities were closed and both companies shared the GWR shed. Then during the Second World War, to increase flexibility of working should one or other line be rendered inoperative due to enemy action, a connection was made between the two routes. Nationalisation saw little immediate change, but in 1951 the GWR station was designated 'North' and the Southern facility 'South'. The names did not last long as in 1952 the GWR station was closed, with all trains now using the Southern facilities; even so, both lines continued to operate independently southwards, the GWR running to Plymouth via Yelverton and the Southern through Bere Alston. After 1952 goods was the only traffic seen at Launceston (GWR), but in this undated view, certainly post-1952, there is little evidence of any traffic, confirmed by the film of rust formed on top of the rails. It was a scene that would become all too common on so many routes as time passed. Notice that, despite the passing of the years, the paintwork is still pure GWR rather than BR's variant of 'chocolate and cream'.

Steam and grime at Stratford on 24 April 1960. By this time steam was very much in decline at this major east London depot. Having once been a builder of steam engines, it was still a major player as regards stabling and maintenance at the time of nationalisation in 1948, with no fewer than 414 engines based there of twenty-three different types. The most prolific were the 124 members of the 0-6-2T 'N7' Class used for the steam suburban services, and thirty-nine 'B12' 4-6-0s used on the main-line services into East Anglia. Just over a decade later the balance had shifted considerably, with 186 steam engines and 196 diesels, the latter mainly Brush Type 2s and 350hp diesel shunters. To complete the picture, in 1963 there was just one steam engine remaining – 'B1' 4-6-0 No 61144. Clearly, then, 'J19' No 64664's days are numbered as its sits and awaits its next move. Having entered service on the Great Eastern Railway to the design of A. J. Hill in September 1918, it was first GER No 1264, then in 1923 LNER 8264, renumbered by the LNER as 4664 in 1946, and finally allocated the BR number 64644 after 1948. Following nationalisation it spent its last years at Stratford and was withdrawn from there in September 1962, one of the last two of the class of twenty-five; none would be preserved.

We see now one of two views taken by Roy of the same engine, both reported as being at Stratford in either 1956 or 1958 – unfortunately we are not able to identify which is which, but it is likely that this is the May 1958 image. Whatever, here is another engine in the last throes of its life. No 65432 is a 'J15' 0-6-0 built to Worsdell's Great Eastern design and placed in service from 1883 onwards. Built primarily as freight engines, several later migrated to branch-line duties, and in direct consequence five of them, including No 65432, were modified to provide some more protection to the locomotive crews when working services over the sometimes exposed Brightlingsea and Colne Valley lines, neither of which had a turntable available at the end of the journey. These changes involved the provision of a side window instead of an exposed cab, and a tender-cab. The latter did not of course prevent all draughts, but it would at least have made tender-first operation slightly more acceptable. The modified engines also had steam heating, vacuum ejectors and balanced wheels, all enhancing their use as both freight and now passenger engines. (Tender-cabs were unusual in Britain. As locomotives got larger so tender heights increased in proportion, and while this in itself might have assisted in providing some protection to the footplate's occupants, the downside was a reduction in view when running in reverse. The Great Western and Southern never had any tender-cabs, while the LMS had a few.) Compare also this side view with that of the other 'J15' depicted earlier in this book, No 65469. No 65432 worked for more than fifty-eight years and was withdrawn in March 1958.

An unidentified 'Castle' blasts its way out of Plymouth North Road station at the head of an 'A' class express on what was a very wet Devon day. The engine is carrying train identification number 623, the purpose of which was to assist signalmen and platform staff in identifying specific trains, any number of which might also be carrying the 'A' class headcode – one lamp over each buffer. Unfortunately the numbers allocated to some services altered over the years in consequence of timetable changes, and in this particular case without a year it is impossible to identify the particular service. Generally trains identified as carrying the numbers 600-699 started from the West Country or Plymouth, while we know that No 620 was the 11.15am Saturdays-only Plymouth-Paddington service. It is possible then that 623 might refer to a relief to that train. What we can say with certainty is that the view was taken in the late 1950s – the later BR crest on the tender and the presence of mechanical signalling at Plymouth confirm this, as the location lost its mechanical signalling very early in the 1960s. Plymouth North Road East signal box containing a 185-lever frame is visible on the right. During the Second World War there had been thirty-one mechanical signal boxes in the area and there were still twenty-seven in 1959 – the four that had closed had their work incorporated into others. Six then closed in 1960, and the remainder gradually faded away so that by 1973 the area of operation of Plymouth panel had expanded to the extent that mechanical signalling in the area was, like the steam engine here, consigned to history. Alongside the right-hand platform are lines of coaches no doubt ready for forthcoming services.

Fowler's 2-6-2Ts were one of numerous steam engine designs that served their owners well, yet were unsung so far as the glamour was concerned (we saw one at Bangor earlier). Seventy engines were built at Derby between 1930 and 1932, taking the number series 1-70 in LMS days and 40001-70 under BR. There were three variations within the class: the basic engines; twenty that were fitted with condensing equipment, where the exhaust steam was passed back into the side tanks to reduce the emission of steam and also to save water; and a few that were fitted for vacuum-operated 'push-pull' use. The latter was a tried and tested operation but, while several railways fitted their engines with condensing gear, if too much exhaust steam was diverted into the side tanks it would raise the temperature of the feedwater too much and in consequence the injectors would not work.

Examples of this class were to be seen on local freight and passenger duties mostly in the London area and the Midlands, although No 40003 was depicted earlier at Bangor and others were recorded at Tebay and Carnforth. The class was fitted with a parallel boiler, although just a few years later William Stanier would take the basic engine design and fit it with a taper boiler to form his own 2-6-2T type. Here Fowler No 40016 is seen shunting at Camden in 1959. It was withdrawn in 1961, one of twenty-two of the class that ceased work during that year.

'Jubilee' No 45666 *Cornwallis* poses outside Crewe fresh from overhaul on 19 March 1960 – we think! (There is some doubt, as the BR crest on the tender was replaced on new paintwork after 1957, so is the date wrong or was Crewe simply using up old stock?) The 'Jubilee' was a three-cylinder version of the Stanier 'Black 5', and 191 were built between 1934 and 1935 concurrently with the other type. All entered BR service, but one, No 45637, was damaged beyond economical repair in the Harrow & Wealdstone disaster of 1952 and not replaced.

In many respects the 'Jubilee' was an enlarged version of the 'Patriot' Class, the first locomotives taking bogies off scrapped LNWR 'Claughton' class engines, withdrawals of the latter class having started in 1929. There were also other modifications within the class, the most noticeable externally being either a domed or domeless boiler and the type and capacity of the tender. At the time the photograph was taken two members of the class had already been withdrawn, but it was not until 1964 that serious inroads were made into their numbers, when no fewer than sixty-six ceased work. One withdrawn engine somehow found its way to Eastleigh among a batch of 'Black 5s' due for repair at the Southern works in the mid-1960s; it should have been sent to a South Wales scrapyard and did indeed eventually reach its destination via this circuitous route. No 45666 lasted until 1965, but was destined not to be one of the four that reached preservation, instead seeing out its last days working from Warrington.

Here is another view of one of the early series of 'Warship' diesels of the D600-604 type, this time at Saltash crossing the approach spans of the Saltash bridge with the station of the same name behind. To be totally honest, this view is very slightly out of the specified time span for this volume, as it is probably c1963-64: witness the small yellow warning panel painted on the front of the loco. In service these engines were capable of running at 90mp,h but that would certainly not be the case over the bridge, nor indeed on the lines in Cornwall where the class was mainly working by this time – again see the earlier image. As was commented earlier, one member of the type managed to survive, albeit vandalised, at Barry scrapyard until 1980, while a spare cab was also in the stores at Swindon for many years after the engines had been withdrawn.

With hindsight, the rush to dieselisation saw several classes of diesel on British Railways have an appallingly short life, and not just on the Western Region. After 1955 there was a rush to place orders and at the same time eliminate steam, whereas a far better option might have been to evaluate a few prototypes before going into quantity production straight off the drawing board. The Western, Eastern and Scottish Regions were probably the worst candidates here, and it would take some years before a corporate policy was established and standard types were seen anywhere from Penzance to Inverness – witness the Brush Type 4s (later Class 47) of later years. The early years of the diesels were thus little different from steam days save for what was actually at the front of the train; it would be almost a generation before multiple units began to be take over almost all passenger workings, their advantage being a quick turnaround at the end of each journey, although suffering the major disadvantage of a rigid fixed formation unable to be adapted for changing daily needs.

This time the bulk of the road bridge over the Tamar is seen almost complete as a 'Warship' diesel comes off the single line past Royal Albert Bridge signal box and the second-man hands the single-line token to the waiting signalman. The signals just visible from the rear to the right of the fourth coach will next be restored to 'on', the token replaced in the machine and '2 beats pause 1 beat' sent by the signalman to Saltash signal box as confirmation that the train is clear of the section. Next the Royal Albert Bridge man will sent '3 pause 1' for the local diesel service waiting on the left, and on receiving confirmation the train may be accepted at Saltash, a token will be released from the machine here and placed in the carrier ready to hand to the driver of the DMU. Then the points will be changed and the stop signal on the right lowered to the 'off' position, although the driver of the diesel will not depart until he has in his possession the all-important token. Notice ahead of the signal box that a new signal has been erected to replace the existing one, the new post and arms carrying an 'X' to indicate that they are not yet in use.

The picture is undated, but as the road bridge, which was started in 1959, is well advanced it is likely to be 1960 at least. The bridge opened in 1961 while in the same year token working was abolished over the bridge – again as explained earlier. Today both the types of train seen are but a distant memory, as is the signalling and the signal box.

This unusual view of Keyham, Devonport, with Weston Mill Viaduct in the distance, is looking west (actually almost north-west geographically) towards Royal Albert Bridge signal box and beyond that the bridge itself, then Saltash station. The '4575' Class 2-6-2T is coming out of or shunting in the Devonport Dockyard link on the left, while on the right the up home signal has been cleared. Two men are standing at the base of the signal, and further ahead on the opposite side of the line are a pair of banner repeaters both showing 'on', thus giving advance warning of the position of signal 56, the down advanced starter, and its associated distant signal worked from St Budeaux. Keyham station is just behind the camera. The image was taken in May 1960, shortly before some changes were made to the signalling in the area. Finally notice the covers in the 'four foot' (the space between the rails) carrying locks for the two turnouts, meaning that passenger-carrying trains might have regularly worked 'wrong road' over what would become facing points.

Probably on the same day Roy has turned his camera around to face the other way and has recorded a Saltash 'motor' (auto-train) leaving Keyham station. Again, the '54xx'/'64xx' engine is sandwiched between the coaches with the driver hidden by shadow in the front compartment. Apart from controlling the regulator and brake (the fireman was expected to lengthen or shorten the valve cut-off as necessary), the driver could also sound the whistle via a cord, and also ring a bell/gong – seen at the top left-hand corner of the carriage front –by the use of a foot pedal. Steam from the engine also obscures the station signal box and also the starting signal. Some years earlier, on 30 April 1941, No 4911 *Bowden Hall* had stopped at the signal box here owing to an air raid, the crew deciding to take shelter under the signal box steps. It was lucky they did for their engine received a direct hit and was subsequently scrapped as being beyond economical repair. Both footplate crew survived. The GWR lost two engines in consequence of enemy action during the war: No 4911 here and a pannier tank, No 1729, at Castle Cary in Somerset, although it must also be said that many others were damaged.

Busy times at Plymouth North Road on 18 July 1957 as a double-headed North of England train blasts its way out of the station behind a pair of 'Hall' Class 4-6-0s. The presence of the two engines is a result of the steep gradients east towards Totnes, and then again from that point through to Aller Junction, west of Newton Abbot. Possibly the lead engine will then be detached ready to be turned and made ready to assist a train in the opposite direction, or it may even work through as far as Bristol, to assist with the climb of Wellington bank between Exeter and Taunton, but certainly no further. The coaches on the service appear to be of LMR origin, confirming the route of the train. Notice the crowds on the platform behind – and this was midweek! On the left a '4575' 'Prairie' is marshalling stock, while at least two other locos are waiting with their trains ready to proceed in the same direction. Signalmen used to say that on days like these they would go home with their meals uneaten as, aside from the regular service, there would be special trains, out-of-course workings and what the Western used to refer to as 'boxers', meaning a short-notice working that was advised from Control to one signal box, which would then pass the information along the line as a 'box to box' notice.

Again slightly out of our time span, but included for the sake of interest, North British Type 2 No D6346 and an unidentified sister engine sit out of use at what is likely Laira. The history of the type has already been referred to, so need not be repeated. Suffice to say that, according to some, they were referred to as 'Baby Warships' due to a perceived similarily in appearance to the D600-604 design, but without the front bonnet. More accurate was a common similarity in internal equipment between the two designs. No D6346 was introduced in June 1962 and had an appallingly short life of just less than seven years before being sold for scrap; the longest-lived was in traffic for just eleven years victims of a manufacturer no longer in business and so unable to provide spares, together with a move away from hydraulic transmission. Indeed, several were withdrawn to provide spares while others were notionally on the books but in store. The similar engine behind is not identified but has clearly been the victim of a side swipe, perhaps therefore awaiting repair or itself ready to yield spare parts. Alongside are several skeletal wagons with clasps ready for ISO containers.

Away from the West Country, we return to Essex and the wooden-surfaced Upminster bay, Platform 1, at Romford. Romford had connections with both the Great Eastern and the London, Tilbury & Southend companies, the latter having a separate station entrance here opposite the Great Eastern facility and a cast-iron footbridge over South Street, which was opened when an LT&SR train was due. This is an early 1950s view, as the 'British Railways' identification is shown in full on the side tank. No 58038 was already then a veteran, having been built by contractor Messrs Neilson, Reid & Co for the Midland Railway in 1876 as an 0-4-4T design. After spending most of its working life in the North Midlands it moved south to Upminster in November 1945 and was then transferred to its final shed at Plaistow in 1948/49. It was the last of what had originally been thirty engines of the 'MR 1252' Class, twenty-nine of which passed to LMS ownership in 1923 and nine into BR hands in 1948. Just three received BR numbers before withdrawal, No 58038 being the final example in service; none were saved for preservation. There was an attempt to close the railway from Romford to Upminster in the 1960s, but this was thwarted and instead it was later electrified. More than half a century later it is part of the London Overground network.

Brand-new 350hp diesel shunter No D3608 was photographed at Stratford on 20 April 1958. Built at Doncaster that year, no fewer than 996 were constructed until production ceased in 1962, thus making the class the most numerous of any BR diesel type. This was also the design that would usurp the steam shunting engine throughout the length and breath of the country, the advantages being obvious in that just one man was required in the cab, the working conditions were far better – warm, dry and draught-free – and the engine itself was able to work literally 24/7 subject to the occasional service and refuelling. No wonder men preferred to work on a diesel! Within the cab the basic driving controls were duplicated, one set on each side, for ease when shunting. Aside from the smart green livery, the wooden cab door may be noted, but it is still some years in the future that 'wasp'-type alternate yellow and black stripes will be applied front and rear to aid visibility for men on the trackside.

A feature of the days of shunting is the provision of the steps front and rear, the latter not just for the use of the driver. However, care had to be taken when a shunter was riding on these steps as he could easily find himself making contact with fixed items such as the point lever seen. Despite the shunting and marshalling of trains being now almost a thing of the past, almost 100 shunters remain on the books of various operators, while around sixty have been saved for preservation and serve a useful role on heritage lines, being able to work at short notice in forming stock. Nonetheless, hundreds have been scrapped. No D3608 was one of these; having been renumbered 08493 in 1974, it survived until 2002, although some reports refer to 2008. Whatever, it was dismantled by C. F. Booth at Rotherham in the summer of 2008.

Notice in the left background the steam loco chassis, seemingly having been adapted as some form of carrier.

No 69585, an 'N2' 0-6-2T to a Gresley design, is fitted with condensing gear and a shortened chimney enabling it to work over the Metropolitan lines to Moorgate. The scene is an unusually quiet Belle Isle, north of King's Cross station, in August 1961, for once devoid of any main-line trains in or out of the terminus. The 'N2' Class and its sister derivatives were the mainstay of the outer-suburban services into and out of King's Cross until replaced by diesels. It was on such workings that the 'quad-art' coaching stock might also be seen – suburban vehicle sets that shared common bogies between the vehicles; this type of carriage articulation saved weight, but meant that the vehicles were stuck in a fixed formation. The practice went out of favour in the 1960s, but was resurrected again for the 'Eurostar' trains in the 1980s.

The smoke-grimed railway is the direct result of countless thousands of trains passing this area for well over a century before the photograph as taken, the grime later added to with diesel exhaust. In the foreground Belle Isle signal box was one of the busiest in the area, passing trains north and south over several running lines. On the left it is possible to see the North London line about to pass over the former GN lines via an overbridge.

Occasional derailments on the line were an inevitable consequence of the operation of the railway, and here we see one such example. There are no details of date or location, but it suggests perhaps Hither Green, as there is some similarity in location to that seen with the derailed No 34084 depicted earlier. In charge of the work is the Bricklayers Arms steam crane, No DS1197, while out of sight would be the riding vans and remainder of the breakdown train. Despite the crane having a theoretical lift capability of 35 tons, much more could be accomplished if the jib angle was vertical. Not obvious is the fact that the crane's outriders will have been extended, and a man positioned on the opposite corner from the lift with the sole task of watching the crane for any sign of the wheels lifting off the rails. Should that happen the lift would be halted at once. Notice also that the crane's counterbalance and boiler of necessity foul the adjacent running line, which will have been 'blocked' by the signalman in charge of it. This is also an electrified area, so it will have been necessary to turn off the 'juice' before commencing the recovery. The vehicle being recovered is a four-wheel utility van and, assuming it is empty, will be well within the lifting capacity of the crane. That said, there were occasions – not here – when complacency ruled and a crane was known to have overturned lifting just an empty four-wheel wagon without the proper precautions having been made beforehand to stabilise the lift.

British Railways in Unseen Colour: 1948-1962

ABOVE AND OPPOSITE Here are two more views of Norwich Thorpe Junction, and from the presence of the waiting steam train being held at signals in the background, they were both taken around the same time. The two-car DMU in the first picture is bound for Norwich and is one of the very successful Metropolitan-Cammell units built in large numbers for BR and formed into either two-, three- or four-coach units. Originating in 1956 with a series of prototypes, the design was multiplied until 1960, the final trains having a service life of forty-seven years. A number have also been preserved. A glance at this image quickly shows the reason for their popularity – wide windows and an open saloon gave an air of space, and provided the driver did not pull down the blinds behind him there was also the interest of the view ahead. Variations included Composite or all-2nd accommodation, and also space for parcels, while there were even a few centre-buffet cars for longer services, with the trains themselves gangwayed between sets. Front-end variations included the provision of a headcode box on the panel above the coupling and 'speed whiskers' on the ends, which to many enhanced their appearance further. As with most of the 'first generation' DMUs, they were of the diesel-mechanical type, and the driver would need to change gear upon reaching a certain speed.

The second image is of English Electric Type 4 (later Class 40) No D203, a great big beast of a machine of 2,000hp and a type used for main-line service as an initial direct replacement for steam on the LMR and ER from the late 1950s

onwards. The type also took over from the 'Britannia' Class on the former GER main lines around the same time. Being 'first generation', though, they were heavy, hence the need to have a carrying axle at the front end of each bogie, while their power output and power-to-weight ratio meant that they were not necessarily the equal of all the steam types they were intended to replace (although that did depend upon the condition of the steam engine, the quality of the coal and, more importantly, the willingness of the crew on board). Here No D203 is attached to at least one Royal Mail coach – unless part of a full train, such vehicles would invariably be coupled close to the engine. Notice also the grime from the brake dust that has adhered to the side of the engine, an inevitable consequence of clasp brakes that were the norm until recent years. In later years this coloured dust would similarly adhere to the more modern blue/grey livery so that even when freshly painted the livery would be shabby within a few days.

No D203 was new in May 1958 and until August 1966 worked the GER lines out of Liverpool Street, being variously allocated to Stratford, Norwich and Ipswich. It then spent a short time at Doncaster before returning to Ipswich until transferred to the London Midland Region. In March 1974 it was renumbered 40003 and survived in service until September 1982, reputedly being withdrawn due to bogie fractures and damage to the power unit. There would be no reprieve and it was scrapped at Doncaster in late 1983/early 1984.

The original 'celebrity' steam engine, born to fame even before modern celebrity status was bestowed (or claimed) by many others, 9F 2-10-0 No 92220 *Evening Star* was the last of a long line, and the last standard-gauge steam engine to be built for British Railways with a basic heritage going back to the days of *Rocket*. The British Railways Modernisation Plan of 1955 decreed that steam would be replaced, perhaps not with the haste as eventually occurred, but new steam construction began to be curtailed fairly quickly afterwards. While No 92220 may not have been the highest-numbered steam engine ever to have been built – that was No 92250 – because the class was built in batches and at different works, so the accolade of the final engine to be completed fell upon No 92220, which was finished and celebrated at Swindon in March 1960. A competition was also held to find a suitable name, and *Evening Star* was suggested by three individuals – a most suitable choice. The engine was enhanced further when it was unveiled during a special ceremony at Swindon and was seen to have been embellished with a GWR-style copper-cap chimney, GWR-style nameplates, a commemorative plaque and a lined green livery – the only member of the class to receive this or be named during BR days.

Ostensibly No 92220 was a heavy freight engine, and 251 of the class were built between 1954 and 1960, quickly proving themselves to be true masters of anything asked of them. (No 92203, when owned by the artist David Shepherd and named by him *Black Prince*, achieved a record of hauling a stone train of 2,158 tons from a standing start at the Merehead Quarry Open Day in 2008. It was reported that the fire was white hot with one-third of a ton of coal and the fireman subsequently had to receive hospital treatment from the effect of the radiant head coming back at him from the firebox.)

Contrary to what had been taken as the accepted norm, the class proved that small driving wheels were not a hindrance to fast running, and when the Eastern and Western Regions tried out the locomotives on passenger trains they were quickly found to be able to run up to at least 90mph. Indeed, there is the lovely story of how a senior Eastern Region man was so impressed with his run up to King's Cross one day that he made a point of visiting the engine upon arrival to congratulate the crew – only to find a 9F at the head. That put a stop to such things in the future. If the class had a weakness it was that it needed a willing fireman – they could burn prodigious amounts of coal if worked hard and it needed a fit man on the shovel. Some members of the class were also tried out very successfully on passenger trains over the Somerset & Dorset line, where their surefootedness made light work of the steep gradients over the Mendip Hills, thus saving on double-heading. Unfortunately, though, they were never fitted for steam heating, so passengers might shiver while the fireman sweated.

The future for No 92220 was thus assured even before her wheels ever turned, and she was saved from scrap for the National Collection. In BR service she was first allocated to Cardiff Canton, then Bath Green Park, Old Oak Common, Oxford, back to Bath, and finally Cardiff East Dock, from where she was withdrawn in March 1965, allegedly having suffered slight collision damage. Including *Evening Star*, nine of the class survive in varying stages of preservation, although it is unlikely that one will be seen operating on the main line in the foreseeable future as the long-coupled wheelbase allied to the flangeless centre driving wheels with which the type were built is not compatible with some designs of turnouts now used by Network Rail.

The engine is seen here on 2 April 1960 at Old Oak Common when just two weeks old and probably having worked up from Cardiff on the up 'Red Dragon' – on one occasion running so far ahead of time that it was deliberately forced to delay its arrival at Paddington to allow completion of restaurant car duties!

An engine from a different era, former Great Eastern 'F4', later 'F5', 2-4-2T No 67193 is seen at Stratford in May 1956, possibly unlikely ever to work again. Between 1884 and 1909 160 were produced, and several lasted into BR days. Compared with the 9F just seen, this design has inside cylinders and inside valve gear, yet the basic principle of coal being used to boil water that is converted into steam and drives pistons still applied. Numerous experiments and alterations were made to the basic idea over the decades, but few were universally adopted, the exceptions being the use of a brick arch in the firebox to deflect the heat, and a taper boiler. But that was not to say steam development was dead, and as late as the early 1960s BR was still experimenting with mechanical stokers, smoke deflectors and exhaust devices such as the Giesl oblong ejector. Sometimes it was difficult to recognise how far development had come, for in the 1950s a batch of 9Fs was built incorporating a pre-heater Crosti boiler intended to boost efficiency and improve steaming, the manufacturer claiming a percentage improvement in double figures. When tested, however, the improvement was single figures and low ones at that, the reason being that the 9F design was already super-efficient for a steam engine and further improvement was notional compared with the changes the same fitting had achieved on older designs elsewhere.

Although coaled and seemingly ready for service, No 67193 looks world-weary and travel-stained and may not in fact have worked again, as it was withdrawn from service from Stratford, where it was photographed, in November 1957.

Cambrian engine, Cambrian scenery. 'Dukedog' No 9017 (formerly No 3217 *Earl of Berkeley*) is on a short pick-up freight 'somewhere' on the Cambrian system. No 9017 was an amalgam of two engines, the frames of 'Bulldog' No 3425 *Sir W. H. Wills* (later renumbered and renamed as 3372 *Sir William Henry*) and the boiler and cab of 'Duke' No 3282 *Chepstow Castle* dating from 1899 (not to be confused with the larger GWR 'Castle' Class engines built from 1923 onwards). This amalgamation, although having slightly less boiler capacity then the 'Bulldog' Class, was as we know a success and the type was a feature of the Cambrian system until the end of the 1950s. No 3217 worked until October 1960 and has spent most of the time since on the Bluebell Railway in East Sussex, far from its original haunts.

The train is a 'K' class pick-up freight, identified by the single lamp above its left-hand buffer. Economics of railway operation have been mentioned before, but we must again question the financial benefit of running just three potentially revenue-earning wagons with three men as the train crew – assuming of course that all the vans were carrying goods. The first van is a BR standard ventilated van of which literally thousands were built. Next comes what looks like an LMS van, with a former SR ventilated van bringing up the rear, all of the 'common user' type. At the rear is a typical GWR 'Toad' brake van, which rarely strayed from the Western Region. The designation 'Toad' was a throwback to the days before the telephone when each vehicle type, and indeed a number of operational requirements, were condensed into a single word or phrase for telegraph purposes, so if for example station 'A' required a brake van it would simply telegraph its name and the words 'send toad'; this saved telegraph and therefore staff time, as well as being clear and unambiguous. 'Toad' brake vans began to fall out of favour in the 1950s as they were not fitted with side lookouts for the guard. Proper GWR practice is, however, being followed as the single veranda was always at the rear of the train, which could lead to brake vans being sent on circular routes in order that they might then face in the correct direction. Notice also the 'pole route' and wires – another long-disappeared feature that once ran alongside the railway.

Ivatt Class 2 No 41302 is replacing an 'O2' on the single line between Bere Alston and Callington some time in July 1961. Notwithstanding the rural nature of this branch line, its condition was no less typical than many others with neat track and ballast, the grass trimmed and the shrubs cut back. All this was down to the permanent way gang, a group of men who were responsible for the day-to-day care and maintenance of the infrastructure between two set points. In addition, and usually each day, the ganger or man in charge would 'walk the length' with a hammer and perhaps a bag of wooden chair keys over his shoulder. Meanwhile the gang would have been allocated a particular task and would congregate probably in the nearest p/way (permanent way) hut – the roof of one such can be seen on the left. (On Scottish lines these were referred to as 'bothies'.)

The time of year would dictate the work involved: track maintenance, perhaps shovelling ballast and packing, during the winter months, and grass and weed control during the summer. For the latter the men would invariably be perched on an embankment or cutting side and would jokingly say that one of their legs was invariably shorter than the other. Working on the p/way gang was one of the hardest jobs on the railway, out in all weathers and with little shelter available, save the warmth and companionship of the tea break in a hut if there was one nearby. In addition the men might be called out for 'fogging' duties in poor weather, when one of them would stand by the distant signal with a detonator, placing it on or removing it from the rail to indicate the aspect of the signal and to help the driver of the train to know exactly where he was in poor weather conditions. They would also deal with snow clearance, all this on top of their usual working day.

This is the main line at Par looking east towards the station and on towards Plymouth. As at Lostwithiel seen earlier, there is an appreciable change of gradient between the main line and the carriage sidings on the left, confirmed by the gradient post on the left. Par was the junction for the Newquay branch, the starting signals for which may be seen on the left by the water tower. Beyond is the commodious goods shed, again similar to that at Lostwithiel. There were three platform faces at the station, serving the up and down main lines and a loop used by branch trains. Opened in 1859 as part of the Cornwall Railway, history has it that the original company considered it too small to warrant a station master, so there was instead a 'booking constable', likely some form of ticket issuer/clerk. Freight was handled until the early 1960s, after which there was a short-lived attempt at a Freightliner terminal on the site of the former goods shed. According to recent figures, Par has seen one of the fastest growths in passenger traffic in recent years with a more than 200% increase recorded since 2002. The signal box is also still operational and besides operating in the immediate area it also has a mini panel to look after the line west through St Austell and Burngullow and beyond.

Here is another view of Keyham and the Weston Mill Viaduct in the distance, this time with a brace of Type 2s approaching with a 'K' class freight. Locomotive headcodes to describe the type of train had been established over many years and it was mainly only on the Southern that route codes were used instead. Consequently in the early days of dieselisation there was no necessity to change what had gone before – the locomotive at the front might be sending out noxious diesel fumes instead of steam and coal smoke – but otherwise not a lot had changed. Digressing slightly, as late as the mid-1980s the steam era was still apparent on the Western Region with a diesel locomotive hauling steam-era Mk1 coaches on Paddington-Oxford-Worcester-Hereford services.

Returning to the picture, we can see one distinct advantage of the diesel era, which was the ability to operate locomotives in multiple as required. Assuming control systems were compatible – and these were identified by a small coloured symbol at each end of the locomotive – control cables were connected in addition to the coupling and brake hoses, and two or sometimes more engines could be operated by a single driver – with steam, of course, each engine would require a separate crew. (As an aside, and not illustrated within these pages, when a steam engine required assistance from a diesel on the Western Region the assisting diesel was always coupled at the front. There were two reasons for this: first, it could be quickly uncoupled when no longer required, but more importantly smoke and ash would not be sucked into the air intake grilles of the diesel. The picture is undated, but from the pristine condition of the diesels it must be around the late 1950s.

East of Plymouth, and close to what was once Plymouth Mutley station (known as 'the station of the gentry' but which, despite that accolade, closed to passengers on 2 March 1939), unidentified 'County' and 'Castle' 4-6-0s have started their journey at the head of what is at least an eleven-coach passenger train – hence the need for the double-heading as it will shortly be starting the ascent of the South Devon banks. Mutley is one of a number of stations that no longer exist on the main line between Plymouth and Exeter, the others (travelling east) being Lipson Vale Halt, Laira, Plympton, Cornwood, Bittaford Platform, Wrangaton, Brent and Exminster. (The original Ivybridge has also closed, although a new station with the same name opened in 1994.) Closure of some of these locations was no doubt welcomed by train crews as they were sited on some of the severest grades of the climb and restarting from a stop on a wet or slippery rail was far from easy. In the background are the approaches to North Road station, with a signal gantry (some might refer to it as a 'signal bridge') indicating to the driver of a down train into which platform he was to be routed. Although undated, we can say – from the carriage liveries and tender crests – that the image was taken in the early to mid-1950s. Another feature assisting the dating is the lack of motor vehicles in Gordon Terrace on the left.

Behind the photographer is the 317-yard Mutley Tunnel. The length of a railway tunnel, on the WR at least, was crucial to the men who maintained the track in the area, for if it was longer than 440 yards is was formerly classified as a tunnel and the men working that area would receive 'tunnel allowance' – shorter than 440 yards and it was a simple 'bridge'. This was crucial to the men maintaining the line at Winchester (GW), some 160 miles east of Plymouth, where there was a tunnel on a slight curve that had been measured at 440 yards, so the men did not receive any benefit. They successfully appealed the decision and had the structure remeasured on the *outside* wall of the curve, whereby it came to 441 yards – they then received their tunnel allowance.

A different use for a breakdown crane at Nine Elms. Under British Railways a panel was set up to decide on historic items worthy of preservation. So far as locomotives were concerned, the selected examples were intended to represent specific examples of loco types, important milestones in design, or machines that had achieved historic importance in other ways. As examples we might cite *Mallard* and, of course, *Evening Star*. Another type represented in preservation was the inside-cylinder 4-4-0, of which numerous railway companies had examples, and a member of the former South Eastern & Chatham Railway 'D' Class, No 737, was chosen. When it was taken out of service in 1956 it was initially stored before being restored to full SECR livery ready for display at what was then the Clapham Transport Museum. To reach there No 737 was towed to Nine Elms, the main locomotive depot for the South Western lines out of Waterloo (and in more recent years the home of the [new] Covent Garden market), and on 26 June 1960, with the aid of crane No DS1561, it was lifted onto a waiting low-loader for the remaining journey to its resting place, the tender travelling on a separate vehicle. As part of what is now known as the National Collection, the engine was subsequently moved to York, where it remains on static display.

Behind are the roofs of the steam shed together with their numerous smoke ducts, while the large black structure on the left is part of the coaling plant.

An early '57xx' series pannier tank, No 7709, leaves Par with a Newquay line freight, possibly destined only for the short distance to St Blazey. From the headcode this is another pick-up freight, and even the first few vehicles represent an interesting combination: a BR brake van (notice the side duckets to allow the guard to see along the train when in motion); a 'Mink' van (another telegraphic description – there were several different types of 'Mink' with a descriptive letter according to size, etc); and at least one milk tanker. Milk was regular traffic from the West Country to the London creameries, the milk tanks themselves being of the six-wheel type to prevent 'hunting' (sideways movement) when travelling full, which might cause the contents to turn to butter en route! The tank has probably been dropped off empty and is on its way back to a branch station or depot for refilling.

No 7709 has the older cab with round spectacle plate windows at the front; later versions were fitted with more rectangular windows. The Great Western preferred pannier to saddle tanks for its small engine designs, as there was easier access to oil the inside motion as necessary. This was also the most prolific class of engine on the GWR, with 863 built between 1929 and 1950, and consequently could be seen throughout the system. In addition there were several other designs that carried pannier tanks., including the '54xx', '94xx' and '15xx' classes, as well as several earlier engine types. A balancing pipe under the boiler ensured that both tanks always held the same amount of water. No 7709 was built by the contractor Kerr Stuart in March 1930 and lasted for thirty years before being withdrawn from St Blazey depot in August 1960. It was scrapped by Cashmore, Newport, in December of that year.

Pride of the GWR passenger fleet were the thirty members of the 'King' Class, the first of which, No 6000 *King George V*, took to the rails in 1927. The type was an enlargement of the 'Castle' Class, which in turn was a development of the 'Star' design, all with a 4-6-0 wheel arrangement and displaying a family likeness that was so typical of the GWR. Seen here is No 6017 *King Edward IV* at Swindon on 10 June 1957, clearly fresh from overhaul. For many years the 'Kings' were based at just a very few sheds, Plymouth Laira, Wolverhampton Stafford Road and Old Oak Common, although they would also be seen at various other depots, notably Bristol Bath Road and Tyseley (Birmingham) being serviced ready for return runs. In the late 1950s they were also allowed through the Severn Tunnel on a regular basis, so also took charge of some South Wales workings. No 6017 is seen here at Swindon in its final form with a four-row superheater and double chimney. Although not visible, the bogie has also been strengthened following fatigue issues in the mid-1950s.

Records indicate that No 6017 had entered Swindon Works on 29 April for a 'Heavy Intermediate' overhaul and was returned to its depot at Laira on 18 June, no doubt having spent a week on 'running-in' duties from Swindon beforehand. The following year it would receive what would be its final 'Heavy General' works visit before ceasing work and being placed in store on 15 June 1962, its duties given over to the new diesel types then entering service in large numbers. The Western Region management was keen to replace steam as quickly as possible, hence all the 'Kings' had gone by the end of 1962, many broken up at the place of their birth, Swindon. Three were saved, No 6000 *King George V* as part of the National Collection, and Nos 6023 and 6024, which somehow found their way to Barry scrapyard and rusted there for several years before being saved in what were major restoration projects. No 6017 ran a reported 1.65 million miles in service, equal to an average of slightly more than 54,000 miles a year.

Green-liveried BR 'Standard 5' No 73055 tops the bank at Camden with a down train in 1959, having just left Euston. As with nearby King's Cross, the start from the terminus was a difficult task for a 'cold' steam engine, with loads (in peacetime) of as many as fifteen coaches on occasions, although records indicate that twenty-plus was not uncommon during the Second World War. The indication here, one lamp under the chimney, is for a stopping passenger train, but even so a substantial load is coupled behind the tender. Colour light signalling is in use, with a ground signal on the right.

Records for the period indicate that No 73055 was based at Glasgow (Polmadie) throughout its life, so seeing it at Camden, 400 miles south, is slightly confusing. At the bottom of the smokebox door a small shed code plate would indicated its home depot, but unfortunately this is not readable in the shadow of the afternoon sun. Possibly it had found its way south on an excursion of sorts and was now making its first tentative steps north and home. From 1951 onwards 172 of this Class 5 type were built by BR and were to seen on all regions, although the majority seem to have found their homes on the London Midland Region and in Southern territory. Generally they were well liked, although at speed they were considered to be harsh riders, while the cabs could also become dusty. No 73055 met its end two years before the end of BR steam; withdrawn in May 1966, it was broken up in January 1967.

Doyen of the 'Britannia' Class, No 70000, awaiting departure from Norwich for London Liverpool Street. Aside from a trace of grey smoke from the chimney all is calm, a good fireman only starting to build up the fire and so raise boiler pressure to maximum as departure time approached, thereby avoiding wasting steam – and effort – as well as causing unnecessary noise. Indeed, at some stations, particularly those in London, there were rules requesting that the emission of steam and smoke be kept to a minimum, not always easy and made even more so should the scheduled departure time be exceeded. No 70000 looks far from pristine externally, but it was the mechanics that counted, of course.

Some passengers are boarding on what is clearly a hot day – notice the droplights down on the open doors. The man on the right may well be a footplateman, dressed as he is blue and carrying what looks suspiciously like an oil can. According to Roy's notes this view was taken in September 1954, but there must be some doubt about this as the smoke deflector handrails have been removed and replaced with hand-holds, something that is believed not to have taken place until after the Milton accident of November 1955. Despite the engine needing a bit of attention from the cleaners, the headcode discs at the front are either new or freshly painted, and indicate a class 'A' express passenger train.

Running on what was often described as 'Brunel's billiard table' – the line was almost level for mile after mile – No 7005 *Sir Edward Elgar* is, appropriately, in charge of a down Worcester service near Cholsey station on 16 June 1957. From Paddington west to just beyond Didcot there were two sets of up and down running lines; the Great Western, its successor the Western Region and even today's operators refer to them as the 'main' and 'relief' lines, whereas elsewhere they would be 'fast' and 'slow'. The main lines are those to the right, No 7005 having already been diverted to the relief in anticipation of 'turning right' at Didcot East Junction to take the Didcot avoiding line and so head north towards Oxford before taking the 'OWW' – the Oxford, Worcester & Wolverhampton route (sometimes cruelly referred to as the 'Old Worse & Worse') – via Honeybourne and Evesham to reach Worcester. The coaches appear a bit of a mixture, as was indeed typical of most WR passenger services, and aside from BR Mk1 vehicles the second coach is a Hawksworth compartment vehicle. On the right the main line has a greater space between the tracks, a legacy from broad gauge days where greater clearance was needed for the 7-foot (and a quarter-inch) between the rails.

No 7005 was among the final batch of 'Castle' Class engines to be built, introduced in 1946 and for most of its life based, appropriately, at Worcester. As built it carried the name *Lamphey Castle*, but had been renamed *Sir Edward Elgar* at the suggestion of the Railway Correspondence & Travel Society earlier in 1957. It is seen here paired with a flat-sided Hawksworth tender, and up to the end of 1962, when records ceased to be kept, it had run in the order of 807,000 miles, or just less than 49,000 miles per year. It finally moved to Southall in August 1964 and was withdrawn surplus to requirements just one month later.

Here is the Lyme Regis branch train again, and this time a 'Bulleid 3-set' makes up the formation. Whether this was the actual branch train, part of the 'Atlantic Coast Express' formation – perhaps unlikely – or simply stock being shunted at the station is not certain, although the engine is displaying the correct single headcode disc for branch trains. The history of Axminster and the branch together with its engines has already been referred to, so suffice to say that in more recent times, from 11 June 1967, the main line through here was completely rationalised with just a single line in operation between Chard Junction and Honiton, a distance of just over 15 miles. This was part of the SR/WR plan to concentrate resources on just the former GWR line between London and Exeter via Westbury and Bristol. At the time, and for some years after, there were fears that the former Southern line might actually be closed altogether, but the whole route from Salisbury through to Exeter has not only enjoyed regular passenger traffic but also growth, culminating in a new 3-mile loop opened in 2009 and involving a second platform here to replace the one previously out of use since 1967. Trains are thus now able to cross again at Axminster, which now enjoys an hourly service. There has even been a limited catering facility resurrected on Waterloo-bound services, operated by a private contractor. Doubling throughout may still be a long way off, but with traffic continuing to develop west of Salisbury one day the railway may once again be a main line, even if the Lyme Regis branch is unlikely to be resurrected.

LEFT 'J15' 0-6-0 No 65361, seen at Stratford in March 1958, has been prepared for snowplough duties. Hard to imagine now, but at most main sheds throughout the country at least one engine would be so fitted in the late autumn and remain ready for use until winter had released its grip – notice the wisp of steam from the safety valves. Each railway company also had its preference as to the type of engine and plough, this particular example being a plough that would push snow to one side only whereas others would literally carve their way through, spreading snow in equal amounts to both sides. The plough has necessitated the removal of the front buffers and pipework, but at least one buffer can be seen standing on the front framing, so this may indicate that the plough will shortly be removed and stored again until the next season. This particular engine was already of pensionable age, having been built in 1889, but it would survive until the end of September 1962.

LEFT 'Small Prairie' No 4565 – in the author's opinion the better-looking version, having the flat-topped tanks – is on a Western Region branch service some time in the 1950s. Unfortunately Roy does not give a date or location, but two possible routes come to mind: one is the Launceston branch from Plymouth, which he clearly visited on at least one occasion, and the other the Moretonhampstead branch from Newton Abbot via Heathfield. Whatever, this was how (G)WR branch trains, other than 'auto' workings, often looked in the 1950s, that is before the widespread impact of the diesel multiple units – a '45xx' or similar, a 'B' set (a two-coach fixed-formation train) and sometimes, although not on this occasion, a van or horsebox, for example.

While branch-line services like these mainly survived into the early 1960s – there were exceptions with lines that closed earlier, such Princetown and Ashburton – it is worth mentioning that as early as 1955 the Western Region at Paddington had prepared a large and detailed report on the 'Modernisation and Re-Equipment' of the railways in the West of England, with particular emphasis on dieselisation of passenger and freight services. In what was a volume running to several hundred pages, the case was made out for rationalisation/closure on a massive scale, with steam replaced and men made redundant, resources being concentrated on a few key locations at the expense of others. Nor was this part of the WR, or indeed BR in general, unique, for the regions were being forced to make a case for modernisation by saving money that could, on paper at least, then be reinvested elsewhere, especially in modern traction. With today's traffic-bound roads, it is easy to question the rationale of the time, but it is also wrong to compare like for like in the same way that decisions being made today may appear wrong when seen fifty to sixty years hence.

Sadly No 4565 is no more, nor are both the branches named earlier. The new concrete sleepers seen here were sometimes cynically referred to as a prelude to closure – 'Paint the station this week and put up the closure notice a week later'.

ABOVE This Stephenson Locomotive Society special to Brighton Kemp Town reportedly took place some time in 1955, but even the excellent 'Six Bells Junction' website appears to have no information. Consequently this may have been a local working just to and from Brighton, as the engine being used is the Brighton Works 'Terrier' resplendent in LBSCR livery. The railway to the terminus here served the eastern side of Brighton, diverging from the main line at the appropriately named Kemp Town Junction. Opened in 1869, it was an expensive railway to construct with a viaduct and tunnel included in what was a branch of just under a mile and half in length. One intermediate station at Lewes Road was opened in 1873. Unfortunately traffic never really developed as had been anticipated, passengers for what was the fashionable area of Kemp Town preferring to use the main Brighton station and continue to their destination by cab or later by street tram. It was these same trams that would force closure in 1932, after which goods continued to be handled until 1971, the station area becoming ever more derelict in the final years. During the Second World War some coaching stock was stored in the tunnel just outside the station, a precaution against enemy action. Today the southern end of the same tunnel can still be found in the midst of the industrial estate that has grown up in the trackless area that was once the station.

At Devonport Albert Road. No 6828 *Trellach Grange* has charge of an up freight train. The use of this engine on this type of train proves the point made earlier as to the versatility of the type, equally at home on all but the fastest or heaviest trains. This type of mixed freight was the backbone of railway services, and indeed revenue, for decades. It was a time when there was little competition save for local goods in primitive motor lorries, and the days of long-distance road haulage were some way into the future. Indeed, the early railways were built on the promise that freight would be the principal revenue earner, with passenger traffic, even if given priority so far as timings were concerned, being very much the bonus. My goodness, how things have changed!

For years the railway suffered under the yoke of being a 'common carrier', which meant that whoever turned up wherever with whatever, the railway had to carry it. This led to a proliferation of different types of goods wagon, some of which were only suitable for literally one or two types of traffic, yet there had been design costs in building it, running costs in operating it, and storage costs when it stood idle on some isolated siding awaiting its next use. Added to this was the business of transporting that load, with the daily pick-up goods collecting from every wayside goods yard – in the case of branch lines perhaps a single wagon a day. Of course the goods yard also needed to be maintained for the same purpose. Then those same goods, or that wagon, would need to be sorted at the main yard, and perhaps sorted again several times en route. To charge the customer correctly and check that delivery had been made, a veritable army of clerks was based at both the country station and in the Railway Clearing House offices if cross-company movement was concerned, and the traffic had to be accounted for at the divisional or head office. Small wonder that British Railways was keen to throw off that responsibility as quickly as possible, concentrating instead on bulk movement of a single commodity to a single destination. The main development today has been the multi-modal container operation, together with a recognition that in some areas rail is best but in others road is more efficient. We are unlikely therefore to see the type of train depicted here repeated in the future.

For the record No 6828 first saw the light at Swindon in February 1937 and was based at Truro between November 1958 and October 1961, so we may date the image between those times. It moved to Oxley, Wolverhampton, after October 1961 and survived until July 1963.

No 4708 was recorded at Plymouth Laira on 17 May 1960. These big '47xx' engines were built by Swindon in 1923, with the majority based at Old Oak Common or in the Midlands. They really were large engines, and designed for one particular purpose, the running of heavy fitted freight trains between major cities, most of which operated at night. Typical duties included bulk workings of perishables, beer, meat and chocolate – almost the forerunner of what we see today in the form of a single commodity to a single destination. The term 'fully fitted' meant that all the wagons were fitted with continuous brakes instead of being 'loose coupled', and as such screw couplings were provided and the train could run at faster speeds – although still taking into account the speed limitations of short-wheelbase four-wheel vehicles.

Fitted with 5ft 8in driving wheels, the same size as a 'Grange' Class 4-6-0 in later years, the '47xxs' were found to be equally capable of passenger work, although this tended to be restricted to holiday relief and summer Saturday workings. Because of their restricted use, just nine were built, but all lasted until June 1962, the last being taken out of service in May 1964. None survived the cull, and the Western Region, intent as it was on modernisation, saw no need to do other than send each for scrap as soon as it was no longer of use. There matters rested until the Great Western Society decided on a 'new build' project, which is currently in progress. Fortunately the general standardisation applied to Swindon's products means that a number of the necessary parts are able to be recycled from engines previous sent to Barry for scrap. These include some driving wheels, cylinder block and axleboxes. A resurrected '47xx' will certainly fill a useful gap in the saved examples of Great Western steam.

Tunnelling was sometimes a necessity in railway construction, either simply because the terrain was too steep to climb over, or because an open cutting would have been impractical. In addition, there were times when the local landowner through whose land the new railway was to be built was simply against a visual sighting of the line and insisted that the railway 'be hidden from view'. At the same time some of the railway engineers of the time were keen to display their architectural skills with examples of their work displayed at the start of such tunnels, such as the western portal of Box Tunnel. How many would see such decorative features is not certain, but in the case of Brunel the high arch was probably as much to calm the early pioneer travellers, who might otherwise fear that the tunnel was far too small to accommodate their train. In the case of a long tunnel, the tops of ventilation shafts might be similarly adorned; the 2-mile Chipping Sodbury Tunnel has a number of ventilation shafts disguised as circular castle turrets, again to appease the Duke of Beaufort. Another tunnel with a distinct architectural twist is seen here, the Grade 2-listed south portal of Audley End Tunnel, looking north towards Cambridge. This 456-yard tunnel was opened in 1845 as part of the GER main line and survives today, the route now electrified. Roy recorded the ornate design brickwork in July 1958.

British Railways in Unseen Colour: 1948-1962

Work-stained and travel-weary, '4575' 'Small Prairie' No 5511 stands at Plymouth Laira in June 1960, just a few days away from a move to Machynlleth – it is possible that No 5511 is being made ready for the trip. The transfer of engines between depots was a commonplace occurrence during steam days, sometimes on a temporary basis to cover for a peak in traffic and other times when engines were being withdrawn and a replacement was thus sent to make up numbers. To the donor shedmaster this could be a welcome opportunity, the chance to rid himself of the proverbial 'lame duck'. Despite a whole class of engines being built to the same specification, using identical parts and components, even in railway experience there was the occasional 'Friday afternoon' machine; indeed, it was rare for the same engine to behave in an identical fashion from one day to the next.

No 5511 certainly looks tired. It is doubtful whether it would have run 'light engine' (without a train of any sort) all the way to mid-Wales, but instead would probably have worked its passage much of the time. Upon arrival in Wales, though, its stay would be brief, for within a matter of weeks it was cast aside, perhaps redundant, or maybe simply in need of some repair that, because of the decline of steam, was no longer being authorised. It was scrapped at one of the South Wales cutting yards in January 1961.

We saw one of the stages of the Locomotive Club of Great Britain's 'Southern Counties Limited' railtour of 24 February 1957 earlier, behind a 'Terrier' tank at Hayling Island. Here, though, we have a view of the train earlier in the day at Clapham Junction, with what was a wet start to proceedings, although fortunately matters did improve later. The engine is No 32424 *Beachy Head*, the front shrouded in steam and with an interesting route code, which is certainly not immediately obvious as it is taking the train to its next port of call at Horsted Keynes. Notwithstanding the conditions, there is a large complement on the platform, some participants possibly joining the train here. Nearly all are all dressed de rigueur for the period with jacket, collar and tie – how things change!

The practice of special trains carrying nameboards was commonplace, while the number of enthusiasts' special workings was also considerable in the heyday of trainspotting. As an example, according to the excellent 'Six Bells Junction' website the number of tours run for enthusiasts in 1957 was as follows: January, five; February, three; March, six; April, twelve; May, seventeen; June, nineteen; July and August, thirteen; September, twelve; October, four; and November, two. None are listed for December, but even so it represents a grand total of ninety-three, with some of them taking place over more than one day. Not all were of course as diverse as this particular trip (described previously), but would often still include unusual locomotives over strange routes. In addition, such trips might take in locomotive works and depots, while the various enthusiast societies would also organise separate site visits to a diverse number of railway installations.

It was a similar story at nearly every main works throughout the country, until the number of withdrawn engines exceeded the capacity of the works to dismantle them; as a result, scrapyards were invited to tender, the tender form usually including a requirement that the engine may only be broken up and not sold on. Carriages and wagons suffered a similar fate and if sent to a scrapyard would inevitably suffer the effects of vandalism before succumbing to the torch. Here No 65432 appears intact, possibly withdrawn for a mechanical reason, or it may simply be that her work had been taken over by a diesel – her secrets disappeared with her.

BELOW In June 1955 at Laira Roy recorded this study of 'Castle' Class 4-6-0 No 5069 *Isambard Kingdom Brunel*, the class member with the longest name (not all were named after historic seats). The engine is attached to a straight-sided Hawksworth tender, certainly not the original pairing, but tenders were interchanged both in the works and occasionally on shed, so this was certainly not unusual. The engine has also recently had its fire cleaned – notice the ash staining on the edge of the cab. No 5069 is sandwiched between two BR Standard types, 'Britannia' No 70016 *Ariel* and Class 4 No 75025, at the time just over a year old and allocated new to the Plymouth depot, having been built at Swindon in April 1954. Both this and the 'Castle' would remain Western Region engines throughout their lives, but No 70016 would transfer to the London Midland Region in 1961.

ABOVE This further three-quarter study of 'J15' No 65432 at Stratford was almost certainly taken on the same occasion as the previous one. This was probably the scrap line, to which engines would be added – or removed – as they made their way towards the inevitable end. Some parts might be salvaged – valves, gauges and the like, or even a set of wheels or bearings if it would keep another of the class in service. Coal and water will also have been emptied out of the tender and the boiler drained, the whole now something in the order of 37 tons of scrap, of which a couple of tons of copper within the firebox was the most valuable component. The tender, all steel and no copper, might also be due to suffer a similar fate, although a few were retained as water carriers, sludge tenders, or for use in a weed-killing train. One item that might be sold is the smokebox numberplate, possible for a few shillings at an Open Day, but not all were saved and many ended up going the same way as the rest of the engine.

The 'Britannia' Class engines were not always popular with Western men, who had been brought up on a diet of Swindon engines with right-hand drive, so it is perhaps no surprise that No 70016 was transferred to Cardiff Canton at the end of 1956, where the class were not only well received but often preferred by crews for the fast London services. No 5069 has a speedometer drive coming off the rear driving wheel, and would later be modified further with a four-row superheater and double chimney. In good mechanical condition, driven and fired well and fed on a diet of good-quality Welsh coal, the 'Castles' were admirable performers, made even better after those latter modifications. They represented a design that dated back to 1923, but was still on front-line duty forty years later.

This unusual view of Chacewater station in Cornwall shows a branch train from Newquay via Perranporth coasting in to the down loop platform. The stock that we can see is unusual in that it consists of non-corridor suburban-type vehicles with, in the middle, a Collett-design Brake with commodious goods/parcels accommodation. At the head is a '45xx' 2-6-2T with flat-topped tanks. The Newquay branch here could be accessed by trains from both the east and west by means of a triangle behind the photographer. Newquay could also be reached via Par, while there was also the freight-only route from Burngullow, which joined the line from Par at St Dennis Junction. On the main line heading west the down starting signal – lower-quadrant, of course, on a wooden post – is in the 'off' position. It is likely a warm day, as on the platform the signalman has the end window of his box open. Signal boxes, with their preponderance of glass, could easily become a like a greenhouse inside, so he may be enjoying some through draught as well. The down train that has been signalled can also just be glimpsed in the distance approaching the station, formed of what appears to be a rake of 'chocolate and cream' coaches.

Chacewater had little in the way of freight facilities, these being confined to the two sidings on the down side where a few wagons are stored. The line in the bottom right-hand corner is the yard headshunt, provided so that shunting could take place while the main line was occupied, but also in the event of a wagon running away it would not foul the running lines. The covers for two facing point locks will be noted, while one bit of minutia we might mention is that wooden signal posts on the GWR were tapered at 1 in 60, meaning a taper of 1 inch all round for every 5 feet of height – hence the taller the post, the wider the base.

Steam suburban workings out of King's Cross are represented by condensing 'N2' 0-6-2T No 69581 working away on a five-car rake of BR suburban coaches, conveniently identified as destined for Hertford North. The fireman has just been, or maybe still is, feeding the fire with some less than ideal coal, judging by the amount of smoke. If combustion is good, which will depend on a number of factors – the quality of the coal, the state of the fire generally, and the amount of coal added so as not to 'black' the fire – any smoke will quickly disperse to leave a light grey cloud at the chimney, so it may be that the crew of this engine are having what every footplateman experienced at times, a 'rough trip'.

The practice of placing a destination board across the front of the engine was common on Eastern Region suburban services but rare elsewhere. The Southern had a number of letter codes on the front of its electric units, which quickly became known to regular passengers; the London Midland did not seem to bother; and the Western expected its clientele to know where they were going. This last aspect was the cause of some names being removed from GWR engines many years ago when folklore has it that a lady passenger boarded a train with the engine named after a town, then complained bitterly when she arrived miles from her intended destination. Rumour also has it that this also happened on the Southern, with a number of engines named after West Country locations.

No 69581 would be ousted on such duties first by diesel locomotives from the late 1950s onwards, then by diesel units, and now the swish efficiency of electrification that has taken over all suburban services out of King's Cross.

ABOVE 'Castle' Class 4-6-0 No 5017 had originally been *St Donats Castle* until renamed as seen here on 26 April 1954. Appropriately, this was a Gloucester-based engine from October 1951 and remained as such until the end of its life on 21 September 1962. Rumour has it (from *The Book of the Castles* published by Irwell Press) that this engine had originally been intended to be *Oystermouth Castle* and the nameplate was actually made when the Chief Mechanical Engineer, C. B. Collett, who happened to be on a tour of Swindon Works at the time, was heard to remark, 'That is a silly name for an engine.' It was therefore rapidly changed. Unlike in some other cases when the removed name was later reapplied to a new build, no more members of the 'Castle' Class were being built by 1954, and *St Donats Castle* simply faded into obscurity. Nameplates were also 'handed', and were lettered 'L' or 'R' on the reverse side. The engine is painted in standard Brunswick Green, sometimes also known as 'Middle Chrome Green', identical almost to the pre-1948 GWR paint colour that was later adopted with much success as the standard colour for express locomotives by all four regions of BR. Of course the Western had to be different, and before the 1950s were out most engines were being painted in green livery…

ABOVE Here is No 65469 – again – and now the reason for its clean livery at Norwich on 31 May 1960 may be explained: it was no doubt being prepared for an excursion special that took place on 11 June 1960. On that day the 'J15' hauled an unusual train of five brake vans, three LMS and two LNER types, forming an enthusiasts' working, the full details of which are not known. What we may say for certain, though, is that the train traversed the route from Thetford south through Barnham (in Suffolk, not the Sussex Barnham) to reach Bury St Edmunds, but where else it had been previously or indeed went subsequently is not known. The fact that the locomotive is running tender-first tends to imply there had been at least one shunt move or run-round en route. According to 'Six Bells Junction', it has been suggested that the special may have been run by the Cambridge University Railway Club; both Oxford and Cambridge had university railway clubs at this time, and would even sometimes unofficially take over the operation and staffing of trains on some remote branch line for the day!

The railway through Barnham had lost its passenger service back in 1953 after some seventy-seven years of operation, and as can be seen here the platform edging has already been cut back. Sometimes this was simply to recover the edging stones, but it could also be because of movements that would otherwise have meant the loading gauge being fouled. (The 'loading gauge' was the all-round clearance needed for a train to safely travel over a section of line.) This could well have been the very last time any fare-paying passengers traversed the route, as it closed completely on 27 June 1960. The red painted coupling rods and guard irons on the tender are not the usual colour, but add a nice touch to the otherwise all-over-black livery.

Electrification of the suburban lines from Liverpool Street to Shenfield was started prior to the Second World War, and ninety-two three-car 1,500V DC train sets were ordered from Metropolitan-Cammell and the Birmingham Railway Carriage & Wagon Company in 1938. Not surprisingly, the conflict delayed matters somewhat, but the system was energised in 1949, although the last of the new trains was not finally delivered until that year. A 1,500V DC supply was then the standard overhead system adopted by BR and was the same as that adopted on the Manchester-Sheffield line via the new Woodhead Tunnel. However, a change of policy by BR saw a preference for a 25,000V AC overhead system, and in consequence new main-line projects were equipped in that way, the first being that from Euston on the former LNWR/LMS main line. In 1960-62 the Shenfield line was converted from overhead DC to overhead AC, and the Shenfield electric sets were converted to work on the new system. We see here what was later designated a Class 306 set passing Stratford en route for Liverpool Street, the '82' indicating the working. These sets were early progenitors of sliding doors for passenger use, something now universal but until then rarely seen outside Underground stock. They were active until the early 1980s, with one set having been preserved.

We now have another Ipswich view – similar to that featuring the Cravens DMU seen earlier – except this time nearer the end of the platform, with the train either on the move or waiting to do so. Two things are of interest here. One is the short arm of the stop signal on the opposite platform, which is set deliberately low so as to be able to be seen from underneath the platform canopy (as described in an earlier image). Also the balance weight and associated components are deliberately on the opposite side of the post between the post and the ladder, the idea being that no one would be injured as they were unlikely to walk between the two. Nowadays 'Health and Safety' would no doubt insist upon barriers and all that goes with them around the structure, even if they were allowed on the platform as they would then restrict the width of platform available to passengers.

In the distance a group of men are working on the track, none wearing the later compulsory orange workgear, but we can be sure there would be a look-out with whistle and flag; also, unless this was an emergency short-notice repair, the driver would have been made aware of track work in the area when he signed on duty. On the right-hand platform the water crane has a 'fire devil' nearby, not needed today but in winter the brazier at the base would be lit and the long chimney placed under the swinging arm in a crude but usually effective means of preventing freezing. In the extreme winter of 1963 there was a tale of a driver of a Stanier 8F who filled the tender tank of his engine with water but it was so cold that the leather bag delivering the water froze solid during the filling process, preventing it from being moved once the tender had been filled. After several abortive attempts to free the item with the coal pick, the driver decided to move the engine to force the bag out of the tender. Unfortunately the result was that the complete water column started to lift up out of the ground, so solid was the ice. It was a saddened driver and fireman who had to declare, for the moment at least, that their steed was as a failure on that particular working.

A Falmouth line train is about to enter the short Highertown Tunnel (or Higher Town Tunnel as it was sometimes known) at Truro. This short 70-yard tunnel was opened in 1859 as the railway progressed ever westwards, and gave access to the Falmouth portion of the Cornwall Railway (not opened until 1863) as well as the line of the standard-gauge West Cornwall Railway. The tunnel was built as double-track, but was initially operated as two separate single lines, one to Falmouth and the other to Chacewater and beyond, until the Cornwall Railway was doubled in 1893 and a junction proper was provided at Penwithers Junction. The engine is a '4575' Class 'Prairie' with the larger side tanks, and the first coach is a non-corridor 3rd Class suburban vehicle with five-or-six-a-side seating – 'cosy' on a warm day.

On the extreme right, and almost hidden in shadow, is a GWR-type 'Limit of Shunt' sign. These were simply worded warning signs, black or red lettering on opaque glass, set in a simple metal frame and illuminated from behind by a standard oil lamp. Their purpose was exactly as the name implies, marking the end of where permissible shunting may take place, often some distance outside a station yard but placed at a sufficient distance to accommodate the length of any train likely to be made up at the nearby station – in this case Truro.

If shunting was taking place on a main line outside station limits, there were strict signalling regulations that applied, one being the 'blocking back' signal, which had to be sent to – and acknowledged by – the signal box in rear, after which the block indicator had to be turned to read 'Train on Line'. This therefore meant that the vehicle or vehicles were protected.

In the opposite direction there was a bell signal for 'shunting into forward section', where a train left a station and was proceeding a short distance into the forward section for vehicles to be shunted. Again special rules (known as 'Local Regulations' and, in the controlling signal box, 'Footnotes') applied, the whole being even more carefully regulated, or totally prohibited in conditions of poor visibility such as fog or falling snow. Every signal box had a 'fogging point', a particular fixed object or structure that if the signalman could no longer see it clearly meant that fog working would then apply.

This 'Limit of Shunt' board has been located here simply because shunting would never be allowed inside a tunnel except in most unusual cases (Winchester Chesil was one such location, where engines were regularly changed between the SR and GWR on up trains, the move taking place mainly in darkness – strict local regulations applied to ensure that the movement was safely carried out). Another reason why a 'Limit of Shunt' sign might be so positioned was where there was a change of gradient, to prevent vehicles from potentially running away.

From main-line engine to diminutive shunter, and here is another example of a small Southern engine (not all Southern engines were small, of course!) in the shape of former SECR 'P' Class 0-6-0T No 31325 seen at Brighton on 30 March 1957. Just eight engines of this class were built at Ashford in 1909-10, intended for light passenger service and primarily as replacements for the SECR's short-lived steam railmotor episode. (The LBSCR and LSWR ventures into steam railmotor vehicles were a similar story, unlike their use on the GWR, where the steam railmotor concept lasted until as late as 1935.) Unfortunately, the 'P' Class design was found to be underpowered for its intended use, and this is likely why the design was never multiplied further, although all eight found a use in shunting and the class passed intact into British Railways days in 1948. Two had also found their way into Government service overseas during the First World War, but again their limited power was a factor and they were returned to England after less than eighteen months overseas.

The first withdrawal was in 1955, then No 31178 was sold out of service to the Bowater paper mill in Kent in 1958. Another was similarly sold out of service to the 'Pride of Sussex' flour mill at Robertsbridge. Due to their limited power, they were never popular on their native SECR, but perhaps because this reputation existed some distance away, there were never any real complaints when one found regular work at, of all places, Winchester City on the LSWR main line, shunting the sharply curved goods yard as well as attaching and detaching vehicles from main-line services.

Here No 31325 (which did not survive into preservation) is depicted on shunting duties at Brighton shed on 30 March 1957, with the local '75A' Brighton shedcode displayed. It is also almost dwarfed by the adjacent standard 16T mineral wagon. This engine had previously been at Dover and Eastleigh; at the former point it would have worked around the docks, while in Hampshire it was probably limited to light work at Winchester, Eastleigh and also Southampton Docks. It was withdrawn in March 1960 and scrapped.

Here is a delightful view of Bodmin General station (the designation 'General' was added after 1949), the terminus of the 3½-mile branch from Bodmin Road on the GWR main line. The practice of naming a station 'Road' was once commonplace, and meant that the station was 'on the road' to a particular place, but deliberately not mentioning how far it might be to the named location. If a railway subsequently reached that town or city, the suffix 'Road' no longer applied and a completely new name might well be chosen to more specifically reflect the location. (An example is what is currently known as Micheldever, where the station was called 'Andover Road' from 1840 until 1856, when a railway did reach Andover.) However, Bodmin Road still survives in 2018 on the main line.

The single-line branch from the main line reached Bodmin in 1887, having to contend with both a steep gradient and a 90-degree turn to head north on leaving the junction. There were no intermediate stopping places, and the terminus boasted all the usual station facilities to accommodate both goods and passengers, together with an engine shed; all the principal buildings were constructed using local stone. A year after opening a second line reached the station from Wadebridge in the west; both lines ran into the terminus so there was no direct through running without a reversal in the station.

In this bucolic view taken in May 1960, time could almost have stood still for several generations. The wooden-post signals and 'Prairie' tank would have been as familiar in 1910 as they were in 1960, while the neatness of the scene was also typical. The engine is involved in running around its freight train – seen in the platform – with the shunter/guard riding on the footsteps. On the extreme left is the line from Wenford Bridge and Wadebridge, while in the middle distance a bracket junction signal shows equal priority for the lines to Wadebridge and Bodmin Road. Nearest the camera the stop signal and 'shunt' signal apply to the single line to Bodmin Road. The engine is probably waiting for the 'shunt' arm to be lowered before proceeding further.

Scenes like this would start to change just two years later when the engine shed closed in April 1962, and passenger services were withdrawn at the end of January 1967. Freight here also ceased from 1 May 1967, and the signal box closed later in the year, although freight from Wenford Bridge continued until 1983. Meanwhile in 1973 there was a slight renaissance when a new siding was added south of Bodmin General on the line to Bodmin Road and wagonload freight was handled for a lighting company until, it is believed, the 1990s. By this time a preservation society had firmly established itself at the station, and today the Bodmin & Wenford Railway is a leading heritage line operating services from Bodmin Parkway to the town as well have having aspirations to return to Wadebridge. It should also be mentioned that there was yet another station in the town; this was Bodmin North (the suffix again being added in 1949), the terminus of the Southern route from Wadebridge, diverging off the Wadebridge line at Boscarne Junction.

Beattie 'Well Tank' No 30585 is seen at the Wenford Bridge clay driers on 19 July 1960. China clay was one of the main exports from Cornwall (was the other clotted cream teas?), with extracted clay from the area first dried before being sent away in wagons either for export or to the Midlands clay and pottery works. Both full and empty wagons are seen in this image, the sides of both liberally doused in the grey/white powder; dried clay has been loaded into wagons that are of necessity then sheeted over – no point in drying the clay for it to become wet again en route. The load behind No 30585 is substantial, even if they are all empty wagons probably returned for refilling; although a strong little engine, a full load of this length would certainly be beyond the capabilities of a single locomotive.

The Wenford Bridge branch was goods only and diverged, as did the line to Bodmin North, at Boscarne Junction. The single line then wound its way over various ungated level crossings and past odd sidings before reaching one of the quarries. Immediately ahead of the engine and painted red is an essential piece of safely equipment, but one that seems to have been rarely photographed, namely a rail-chock. This was locked in position across one rail to halt the progress of an uncontrolled wagon or train should it reach this point, when derailment would invariably occur. The chock could be unlocked and turned through 90° so as to be parallel with the outside of the running rail when it was clear to proceed.

Roy's notes for this view are somewhat limited: 'No 62052 in the Highlands April 1961'. Fine, but where? The local knowledge of the individual reader may assist here, but the obvious choices without conviction are either the West Highland line or that to Kyle of Lochalsh. Whatever, we will instead turn our attention to the locomotive, a Peppercorn 'K1' 2-6-0, seventy of which were built between May 1949 and March 1950, the last engines built to an LNER design to be delivered to British Railways. The 'K1' design was actually based on a slightly earlier rebuild by Peppercorn's predecessor, Edward Thompson. Many of the class were based in Scotland, and while we tend to think of the BR Standard types having short lives, this was another class that suffered the same fate, all being withdrawn between 1962 and 1967. One was saved, No 62005, originally purchased principally as the source of a spare boiler for the already preserved 'K4' No 61994; however, it was later donated to the North Eastern Locomotive Preservation Group, which was able to restore the whole.

No 62052 was allocated to March when new in November 1949, but moved north to Glasgow Eastfield in March 1952 and from then on spent the remainder of its life in Scotland, from May 1954 based at Fort William, exactly the right place for the West Highland line to Mallaig. It was withdrawn for scrap at the end of 1962 and did not survive, although it lay moribund for nearly sixteen months before being cut at Cowlairs. Here it has a four-coach load, two at least being BR Mk1 vehicles, and carries the 'A' class headcode.

THE ARCHIVE

This was another location that led to some head-scratching, with no help from the index, but it turns out to be Doublebois on the Cornish main line, looking west towards Truro. There is an awful lot of interest in the photograph, which first provided the clue that it was certainly a GWR line. Behind the photographer is an overbridge or other structure, as it will be noted that the stop signal has a sighting board behind the arm – painted white on the reverse – which will assist the driver in viewing the signal aspect against an otherwise similarly coloured background. Sometimes sighting boards were little more than an area of white painted bricks on a bridge, and while mechanical signals are a rarity today their previous position can sometimes be imagined from an area of fading white paint on an otherwise red-brick overbridge.

The main line here is on a steep down gradient, hence the angled board to the left of the wagons, which, although unreadable here, will say something like 'All down goods and unfitted trains must stop here to pin down brakes'. This the driver and guard have already done as the engine at the head can be seen to be working against the pull of the brakes to take the train towards the stop signal in the distance. Behind the camera is also a signal box, its position indicated by the point rodding running along the right-hand side. In the yard – the level of which gives a clue to the severity of the steep downhill gradient – there has clearly been little movement for a few days, the surface of the rails being covered in rust. A ringed 3-foot signal protects the exit on to the running line, while a catchpoint is also just visible. The solitary wagon is due for repair; its roof is leaking, hence the tarpaulin stretched across the top. It is a sylvan scene, one no doubt seen elsewhere countless times.

At 'Top Shed', King's Cross, in July 1961 the influence of diesels is beginning to show – just. Otherwise it is steam through and through with at least three members of the beloved 'A4' Class visible – one has its 'Cod's Mouth' (the casing in front of the smokebox door) open, while there are also numerous examples of contemporary Eastern Region steam including locomotives of 'A2', 'A3' and 'V2' types. Note also the 'Britannia' under the coaling stage. The latter dominates the area to the left with both full and empty wagons nearby to feed the monster. On the extreme right workmen have hung their outdoor clothing on the end of the buffers of a wagon, while in the distance and on the right is a part of King's Cross goods.

A 'Modified Hall' approaches the station at Plympton with an up 'A' class working, and from the coaches, another through working to the Midlands. It is possibly also a relief service, as there only appear to be six coaches. Apparent is another example of a stop signal with a sighting board, the up home, and its position on the opposite side of the line is necessitated by the curve on the approach. In the goods siding a gang of p/way men are attending to the crossing, and from the look of it the tie-bar holding the blades together is receiving attention. Another short 3-foot ringed arm guards the exit from the up refuge siding

On the extreme left is a concrete warehouse raised above the ground. Often these were used for the storage of grain or sacks; the West of England Sack Co had depots at a number of railheads, and hired sacks to farmers at different times of year. The grain residue in the returned sacks would attract vermin, hence the need to raise the structure off the ground and support it on what was the modern concrete equivalent of staddle stones. Attached to the wall of the building is what is probably the statutory warning board cautioning about climbing on to the roof, likely ribbed asbestos sheets, which should not be walked upon but crawling boards used instead to spread the weight. Finally, just in view on the extreme right is the sign for a permanent 60mph speed restriction on the main line.

ABOVE It is summer time on the Looe branch and a three-car Western Region DMU heads back up the branch from the riverside terminus towards Moorswater, where it will reverse before attempting the final ascent and steep curvature to the junction station at Liskeard. 'Speed whiskers' are present, although an old-fashioned oil tail lamp is in use; even though it is daylight, a tail lamp was a prerequisite on the last vehicle of all trains.

This branch was one of almost all the rural routes in the West Country to be considered for closure in late 1955, justified by the fact that the traffic was seasonal and between October 1954 and May 1955 there were only an average of seventy-two passengers per day. An alternative bus service was also already available. Freight traffic to Looe was also considered to be small and the WR's conclusion was that the line should be closed completely between Moorswater and the terminus. Nothing was done, however, until the time of the Beeching Report, which also recommended closure, intended to take effect in 1966. At the eleventh hour Transport Minister Barbara Castle intervened and today the railway is thriving with an average of more than 300 people using the line daily every day of the year. (A similar recommendation to close the line between St Erth and St Ives was refused by the Minister at the same time.)

TOP RIGHT '43xx' series 2-6-0 No 7317 stands at Laira in July 1961, and from the look of it it is some time since it was last visited by the cleaners. The '43xx' type was introduced by George Jackson Churchward from 1911 onwards, with no fewer than 342 built in batches up to 1932. No 7317 appeared in December 1921 and would have a life of forty-two years. As with the pannier and 'Prairie' tanks, examples were to be seen throughout the GWR system and, while not entrusted to the fastest or heaviest loads, they were often to be seen slogging away at the head of a freight train weighing hundreds of tons, at the same time rocking gently from side to side as each cylinder took a charge of steam. If working hard on a passenger train this rocking could also translate to a fore-and-aft motion imparted through the coupling and buffers to the first two or three vehicles; knowledgeable travellers therefore made their way to the centre or rear of a long passenger train if there was a two-cylinder engine at the head. The design was a total amalgam of standard parts, hence specific components, which were always stamped with the number of the receiving locomotive, might be identified as coming from any one of a number of tank or tender engines.

Between 1936 and 1939 100 of the earliest engines of the class were withdrawn and several of their major parts used in the construction of the more modern 'Manor' and 'Grange' types. The intention had been to eventually withdraw all the class for conversion in this way, but war interrupted and after 1945 the idea was never resurrected. Consequently a considerable number lasted well into BR days, the last four being in service until 1964. At the time No 7317 was photographed it had worked south from its home depot at Bristol St Phillips Marsh (82B) and would no doubt soon be taking up its allocated return working. Two of the class have been preserved.

BOTTOM RIGHT Eastern Region Departmental Loco No 32 is seen at Stratford in May 1958. Originally Great Eastern No 281, then LNER 7281, 8370 and BR No 68370, it was transferred to departmental service in September 1952. Departmental locos were those allocated a specific non-revenue-earning task, sometimes at a specific location, which might be shunting at a works or similar work at a dockside or perhaps sleeper depot. Usually they were chosen for their short wheelbase, improving their flexibility. Originally fifty of the 'J66s' (the LNER classification) were built, intended for shunting. Dating from 1885/86, it was not surprising when at around fifty years of age withdrawals started, although ten years before this in 1926 four had already been sold to Sir Robert McAlpine to assist in the construction of the Ebbw Vale steelworks. By 1948 eighteen were left, but by 1955 there were just three, with No 32 the final survivor, being consigned to scrap in September 1962. Departmental number 32 was resurrected shortly afterwards and given to a 'B1' allocated to carriage heating. The reason for the 'X' on the chimney is not known, possibly marked for component replacement.

187

For our penultimate view of Inverness, Roy has turned the camera around past the coaling stage to show the archway in front of the semi-roundhouse steam shed on the left. It would interesting to speculate how many engines might have passed through the archway over the years, each adding to the build-up of soot on the stonework. As to why there was such a magnificent edifice forming the entrance to what was simply a place to service engines is probably lost in the mists of time, although on occasions such structures were intended to impress others with their supposed wealth, grandeur and status, in exactly the same way that a stately home might.

The roof of the passenger station can just be made out above the engine shed (or 'engine houses' as they were colloquially known in earliest days). Of the engines seen in the distance, three, judging from their tenders, appear to be 'Black 5s', the other possibly a BR Standard type. Aside from its own allocation of machines, engines would arrive for servicing from other depots dependent on their particular duties. In this way engines might visit from places such as Aviemore, Perth South, Kittybrewster, Helmsdale, Forres, Keith, and even as far north as Wick. In 1948 some sixty-six locos were based here, mainly ranging from former LMS and Highland Railway designs but later to be joined by various BR Standards.

LSWR 'M7' No 30035 arrives at Bere Alston form the Plymouth direction with what is a short working from Friary to Tavistock North – the suffix distinguishing the LSWR station from its GWR neighbour. On the right is the single-line branch dropping down from the loop platform towards Callington, with the signals and sidings referred to earlier. No 30035 has five coaches in tow; at the front is an LSWR vehicle with certainly what appear to be at least two Bulleid-design vehicles behind. There is no date for the image, but it is certainly some time before February 1960, when the engine left the West Country for good for Eastleigh then Nine Elms and finally Feltham.

Bere Alston was on the Southern main line to Plymouth, running via Exeter Central, through Exeter St David's and thence via Crediton, Okehampton, Tavistock and Bere Alston. There are three things of interest in the image. The '683' plate is the bridge number; all structures along the line from the most inconspicuous cattle creep to viaducts, overbridges and underbridges and even footbridges were identified by a number, which started from Waterloo, but would then change dependent upon the line concerned. Hence there could be, say, a No 333 on both the West of England line and the Bournemouth line, but the location would give the exact place referred to: 'Bridge No xxx near xxxxx station'. Next look at the two warning notices, one lettered 'L&SWR' and the other 'Southern Railway'. Usually these would have white lettering on a green background, but it is almost certainly white on chocolate – has the influence of the Western Region been that rapid?

To the right of the first coach there is a gangers' trolley hut, where a motorised inspection trolley might be stored until needed. Such trolleys had two functions, the first being to enable an inspection of the line to take place far faster than was possible by walking – although the ganger was still expected to walk the line at least once a week – and the second being to transport men and tools to a work site, again far more quickly than could be achieved by walking. The trolleys were light enough to be removed from the track by four men. Naturally they were signalled between signal boxes using a special code, as they were railed vehicles.

Incidentally, Exeter St David's was one of those stations where a passenger might, and indeed still can, leave for London by trains travelling in opposite directions, the Southern line heading almost south before turning east through Exeter Central and thence via Salisbury, and the Great Western line running north, then slowly east to travel via Reading.

LEFT We visited Mary Tavy & Blackdown station early on in these pages to see a passenger train, so here at the same location in May 1960 '57xx' pannier tank No 3686 is in charge of a down freight consisting, it seems, mostly of containers and vans, but with one grain wagon midway as well as two open wagons. The weight is difficult to confirm as it will of course depend on the loading of the vehicles, but it could be as little as 200 tons or anything up to double that. Whatever, No 3686 does not seem to be having any difficulty, with no obvious effort or steam showing. As was stated earlier, the GWR Launceston line was in very close proximity to the LSWR Plymouth-Okehampton line at this point, the course of the latter identified by the parallel fencing across the field to the right. The wagons with containers were an early method of moving goods by both road and rail, transhipment being possible at most stations through the use of either a fixed or portable crane – but obviously not here at Mary Tavy & Blackdown! On the right are what are undoubtedly railway cottages, the distinguishable style recognisable wherever one went and often, of course, placed conveniently close to the railway. The train may well have picked up the various wagons at any number of stations on the way down, and they will then be sorted or stabled at Tavistock Junction yard, either for forward transit or to be stored until needed again. Today both railways are no more, although there is still hope that one way the 'missing link' between Okehampton and Bere Alston may be restored.

The train is also seen from the rear, and the proximity of the Southern line is even more clearly defined in that view. On the SR route it is also possible to make out a concrete permanent way hut, one of the many products of the Exmouth Junction concrete works; countless hundreds of this type of structure were turned out for use throughout the former SR system, made in sections and craned into position on site. Some were also later recovered from closed lines for use elsewhere. Just visible on the rear of the brake van are two of the three lamps that were carried on this type of freight train, one on the rear and one on each side of the vehicle. This particular brake van also has a vacuum brake pipe.

ABOVE 'Patriot' Class No 45510 was photographed on Camden bank and, with a tender full of coal and the tail lamp on the front, is probably waiting to back down to Euston ready to take a train north. It was based at Willesden from 1955 until 1959, so it is likely that this view was taken shortly before it moved north to Carnforth, then subsequently Carlisle and finally Lancaster. It was also one of the few members of the class that never carried a name.

The class had its origins in two rebuilds of the former LNWR 'Claughton' type and was based on the chassis of a 'Royal Scot' but with the smaller boiler of a 'Claughton', hence the obvious nickname of 'Baby Scot'. (As we have seen earlier, a similar amalgam had occurred with the 'Dukedog' combination on the GWR.) Fifty further engines were built up to 1934 and, while capable of good work, so far as the enthusiast fraternity were concerned they were often overshadowed and indeed overlooked in favour of the more glamorous 'Duchess', 'Princess', 'Royal Scot' and 'Jubilee' types. This was both a pity and unfair discrimination, for the engines continued to perform well up to the demise of the rebuilt engines by 1965 although all the original engines had gone by 1962. None were saved. However, that oversight will hopefully be put right in 2019 when a 'new build' appears. As an indication of the interest there has been in resurrecting the design, the frames and cab are already complete and work progresses apace on the remainder of the engine.

A down mixed freight is seen at Harlech, on the former Cambrian main line between Machynlleth and Pwllheli. In the 21st century it would a rare sight indeed to see a freight train on this line, but 60-plus years ago in 1957 a '22xx' type would have been common on both passenger and freight workings. The ten vehicles would prove little problem for this engine; indeed, there is a sign of good steaming, a 'feather' from the safety valve. The photograph was taken from the height of Harlech Castle and shows off the type of engine well; they were designed for just this type of duty, secondary and branch-line working. The class replaced the earlier 'Dean Goods' 0-6-0 design on several duties, but only because of age; indeed, some members of the earlier Dean design soldiered on into BR days. The '22xx' or '2251' Class as they were variously known consisted of 120 engines built between 1930 and 1948; they were also sometimes known as 'Baby Castles', as there was a similarity in the cab design. None were ever named, but one member of the class, No 3205, survives.

All ceased work between 1958 and 1965, the latter year seeing the end of Western Region steam, when the locomotives were in a terrible state both externally and internally, yet were still sometimes called upon to deputise for a failed diesel. Indeed, at one time diesel reliability got so bad that management instructed that public announcements of delayed trains due to failure were not to include the word 'diesel', as this would be seen as a snub to the more modern traction. Unfortunately it is not able to identify the specific locomotive seen here, but it may be worth mentioning that towards the end of their lives some were painted in pseudo GWR green at Swindon. Finally notice the occupation foot crossing at an angle in front of the engine.

Back to west Cornwall again now for this view of No 5522 stabled in the goods shed road at Par awaiting its next passenger duty some time in October 1957. The coaches are both in 1950s BR red livery, yet the difference between the colours is remarkable, with one in faded service livery and the rear vehicle having more recently left the paint shop. Much debate exists among enthusiasts, and in particular modellers, concerning the correct shade of red that was used, yet here are examples that would no doubt cause even further debate. The first vehicle even appears to have a chunk of red missing – it is not a blotch on the original slide! No 5552 was then a Truro-based engine and worked until October 1960, being made redundant as a result of the influx of diesel units.

Visible in the background above the roof of the second coach is the loading gauge, an item that has been mentioned before but not illustrated. Basically, if a goods wagon was loaded and there was doubt as to its height or sideways overhang, it would be shunted under the gauge, and provided that the latter did not move or the load was outside the width extremities of the arm the wagon was clear to travel. Outside these parameters it could well foul structures along the route. As the railway system was made up of a large number of company amalgamations, absorptions and takeovers, so the loading gauge varied between different lines – the former GWR broad gauge lines were among the most generous anywhere.

British Railways in Unseen Colour: 1948-1962

A type not seen in detail yet is the LNER 'K5' (originally 'K3') 2-6-0. No 61863 of that class is recorded at Stratford in March 1958, coaled and seemingly ready to have steam raised. Built in 1925 and intended for freight work, the class was the equivalent of the GWR '43xx' and SR 'Moguls', and could also sometimes be seen on passenger working. No 61863 was unique within the class having started life as a three-cylinder machine but rebuilt in 1945 with just two outside cylinders of the 'B1' type, a new boiler, frames and wheels – in fact, very little of the original engine remained, hence the reclassification to 'K5'. Trials in its new form were good and plans were made for a further ten conversions. Running sheds reporting improved riding, greater adhesion and the major benefit of easier access for maintenance compared with the previously restricted space to attend to the inside middle cylinder. Unfortunately the schedule for the additional conversions was cancelled in 1949 and No 61863 thus remained the sole example of 'what might have been' until withdrawn from traffic in June 1960.

As an aside it might be worth mentioning that the use of two cylinders instead of three or four was indicative of what would happen – with a solitary exception – when the BR Standard designs began to appear from 1951 onwards. Two outside cylinders were considered far easier to access and maintain compared with the cramped layouts invariably associated with inside-cylinder designs. The exception in the Standard range was the solitary No 71000 *Duke of Gloucester*.

No 61605 *Lincolnshire Regiment* was a member of the 'B17/6' Class, more commonly referred as 'Sandringhams' or 'Footballers'. This engine had originally been named *Burnham Thorpe* but had a name change in April 1938. Another change, more practical than merely aesthetic, was the fitting of an LNER '100A'-type boiler in January 1948, which led to the change in class designation from 'B17' to 'B17/6'. A few years earlier, in September 1937, two members of the type, then LNER Nos 2859 and 2870, were streamlined in similar form to the well known 'A4' Class, so that they might be used on the named 'East Anglian' train. The embellishment was solely for publicity purposes and probably had little effect on the actual speeds achieved, and by 1951 the pair had reverted to the conventional appearance.

The cascading effect of new engines replacing earlier designs resulted in the class being replaced on many of the services to and from East Anglia by the 'B1s', which were in turn been superseded by the 'Britannias'. Consequently the first three were withdrawn in 1952/53, and all seventy-three were extinct by the end of 1960. None survived into preservation, but several of them that were named after football clubs, which had a nameplate consisting of a football and the club name, are still recalled as the plates were sometimes presented to the club concerned. No 61605 was built in December 1928 at the Gorton (Manchester) works of the former Great Central Railway, by then a constituent of the LNER. It was photographed at Stratford on 20 September 1952, and lasted in service until May 1958.

British Railways in Unseen Colour: 1948-1962

In this last look at Wadebridge we see a Western Region pannier tank, No 4666, hurrying into the station with dark-liveried SR Maunsell stock. This may well have been a shunt move, as the guard can be seen leaning from his window – notice too the side ducket (look-out) ahead of him, which he could use to observe where the train was en route. (The guard's responsibilities were not restricted to simply blowing a whistle and waving a flag at stations – he was also expected to observe signals when possible and generally check that all was in order during the journey.)

Mention has previously been made of the line between Bodmin General and Wadebridge and here is proof of workings between the two with the 'Toad' brake van announcing its 'Bodmin General' home station. The letters 'R.U.' stood for 'Restricted Use', meaning that the vehicle was not 'common user' and therefore should remain within the locality or perhaps be restricted to a specific duty.

From Wadebridge passengers could venture to Padstow – the furthest outpost of the Southern from Waterloo – to Bodmin General or Bodmin North, or north and east towards Launceston, Halwill, Okehampton and eventually Exeter, Salisbury and London (by the Southern route, of course). Indeed, apart from the engine and brake van the scene is 100% Southern, the signals, concrete footbridge and canopy all being to that company's designs. After more than 130 years of service Wadebridge station closed in 1967, the Southern route north around Dartmoor having succumbed the previous year.

This final LNER loco view shows condensing 'N2' No 69531 at Wood Green on the main line north out of King's Cross in September 1958. Whether the engine was shunting or attached to a local working was not reported. A description of the history of the class was given earlier, so need not be repeated here, but instead in what is an excellent side view we may concentrate on some of the engine's fittings, many of which were also common to other steam locomotives. Slightly to the left of the cab steps is one of the injectors, used for putting water into the boiler, using boiler-pressure steam to do so. To achieve this the fireman would first turn on the water supply, which would immediately start to run out of the exhaust pipe seen disappearing behind the lower step. Next he would turn on the steam valve adjusting both until neither steam nor water was escaping from below – easy to see in daytime but not so easy at night. This would be accompanied by a gurgling sound indicating that the water was indeed entering the boiler. When the required level of water had been injected, by reference to the boiler water gauge, the supply of both steam and water would be turned off. Care had to be taken to ensure that the water level was not too high, as water might otherwise be carried over to the cylinders with potentially disastrous results – steam can be compressed but not so water!

Notice too the various handrails for use by the fireman, cleaner or fitter. There was a small ledge in the running plate to allow a man to make his way round, but it was narrow and there was a need to avoid various parts – railway engines tended to bite back if a shin or another part of the anatomy came in contact! Finally there is a sand pipe ahead of the front wheel, running down at 45°, while another to the rear driving wheel is almost completely hidden by the footsteps. These would, under the control of the driver, deposit sand on the rails to help with grip – steel on steel was not always the best combination. All these items were repeated on the opposite side. The engine has also had some slight bodywork damage to the corner of the bunker, but certainly not enough to take it out of service.

No 69531 was built as Great Northern Railway No 1752 in March 1921, became LNER 4752 in March 1924, then 9531 in August 1946, and finally BR 69531 in November 1949. At the time of this photograph it was allocated to Hornsey, where it had been for some time. After 1959, however, there came a series of moves, all short-term, first to Hitchin, then Hatfield and Grantham and finally New England (Peterborough), from where it ceased work in July 1961.

LEFT These are two most interesting and unusual images, one especially giving a rarely recorded view of a Southern Region 'Q1' on an inter-regional working from the Southern Region to Temple Mills yard near Stratford, seen passing through Lea Bridge station. The train will have taken a route from the SR to Willesden, then east through to Highgate and Tottenham before making its way through Lea Bridge, close to its destination. Eastern Region engines also sometimes working in the reverse direction. This type of working was necessary to transfer wagons from one region to another, similar transfers occurring between the Southern and London Midland at Willesden and the Southern and Western at Old Oak or Acton – and that was just the transfers that took place in the London area!

The 'Q1' Class was the brainchild of the charismatic and far-sighted Chief Mechanical Engineer of the Southern Railway, Oliver Bulleid, whose engineering ideas for steam were perhaps, shall we say, a bit too radical for British Railways at times. However, his 'Q1' was a successful design without frills and able to haul prodigious loads. If the locomotives had a fault it was simply that they had insufficient brake power to stop the sort of train they could pull! But then they were intended to work with trains that were either all vacuum-braked or formed of at least some continuously braked vehicles. Unfortunately we cannot identify the specific engine from the forty-strong class, but several were shedded at Hither Green specifically for this type of duty, while others could be seen working from Feltham as well as elsewhere in the SR London area. The headcode of two discs indicates that this train is indeed at least partly fitted with continuous brakes and is a BR standard headcode rather than a Southern Region route code.

Lea Bridge station opened back in 1840 on a line with an unusual 5-foot gauge, but it was changed to standard gauge (4ft 8½in) in 1844. Passenger traffic continued until 1985, although the route itself was an important link and continued to host inter-regional trains, albeit most now the Freightliner type or single-commodity bulk workings. Development in the area created a call for the passenger station to be reopened and this occurred from 16 May 2016, although by this time all that was left were the up and down running lines, goods having ceased at the end of 1970. There was also a private siding into a works area, which is seen being shunted.

In the second view an Eastern Region Brush Type 2 (with a headcode box above the cab) is making its way north on the relief lines that were used by freight, and also provided direct access to Temple Mills. The large-small-large window arrangement of the diesel cab was to allow for access doors at the front, through which a crew member could pass to a similar locomotive if two were working in multiple. Several of the early diesel designs had this type of feature, which was considered necessary at the time but was found to be seldom used in practice.

ABOVE Our final view of an ex-LMS locomotive is this former Caledonian 0-4-4T shunting at Inverness – we saw it earlier at the same location, but here it is in close-up and in remarkably clean condition. One of the disadvantages of an overhead coaling plant is also visible in the form of coal liberally sprinkled on the cab roof; in a shed or yard area such a situation was not a problem, but if No 55160 was to venture out on to the running lines it would be essential that this be swept off as a lump or two becoming dislodged en route might have serious consequences.

This was possibly an organised shed visit, judging by the number of individuals standing on the left. Notice too the signal box, stained with smoke and soot, on the right. In the yard beyond there is an old coach long out of passenger service but now perhaps in departmental use, or perhaps even in use as a store or mess room. This was something that was once a commonplace sight on the railway when yards were aplenty, but a sight that, like the steam engine, is fading fast from memory. To see a shunting engine is such a condition was not always unusual, as it might be in regular use as the shed/station pilot and could become something of a celebrity – as indeed happened at Liverpool Street, York, and Brighton Works. But whatever following No 55160 might have gained was not enough to save it from the inevitable and it was withdrawn and condemned in October 1958 and cut up for scrap soon after.

For our final series of views we are once again visit the Western Region. Obviously Roy travelled widely, and while there are some records of his trips from the photographs he took, it must also be said that not all the images from his listings appear to have survived. Here is one from a location he appears to have visited just once, the now long-closed station at Uffington between Didcot and Swindon. This was the junction for the Faringdon branch, seen diverging on the left, but which lost its passenger service at the end of 1951, long before the days of Dr Beeching. The train is a local working between Didcot and Swindon, calling at the intermediate stations of Steventon, Wantage Road, Challow, Uffington and Shrivenham, all of which have long closed, although the main line still exists and is today traversed by HST and IEP sets at speeds that could simply not have been imagined back in the 1840s when the railway first reached here. Unfortunately, at Uffington withdrawal of the passenger and goods facilities and demolition of those wonderful Brunel-era station buildings came too early for preservation or listed status. To BR's Western Region management, in its shiny new divisional offices at Reading, redundant assets were just that, redundant, and a special department was charged with the disposal of items as quickly as possible, for as much as possible. The railway had to pay rates on structures so buildings were sometimes the first things to be levelled. Consequently there is now nothing left at the site of Uffington station, although the house on the right still exists.

The engine in its dirty livery and accompanying shabby maroon coaches is also hardly the image of the modern railway. Possibly the '61xx' tank engine is making its way to Swindon for overhaul, the stopping service being a good way of earning some revenue with it. Perhaps it is going for scrap, or perhaps its condition was the standard of the time. Small wonder that people welcomed the modern look of the new diesels, a new era and the promise of better things to come – how often have we heard that same phrase over the past fifty years in relation to railways…?

Former Swansea Harbour Trust No 5, later GWR No 701, then 1140, stands in a line of other small shunting engines at Swansea in either 1955 or 1958 (Roy has two entries for the same image with differing dates). On the left is No 1152, another 0-4-0ST built for Powlesland & Mason – a small company taken over by the GWR – and on the right No 1144, also from the former Swansea Harbour Trust. From the rust on the wheel treads No 1140 at least may have been out of service for a day or two, but certainly not long enough for any corrosion to have formed on the piston rod, which should have a film of oil on it anyway. It is interesting to note the slight variation in the height of the buffers between all three engines; such variations coupled with sharp curves and uneven track could often lead to derailments when propelling vehicles, although as most of these would occur at very slow speeds the shunters were dab hands at rerailing where necessary, often using just a few chunks of wood rather than the heavy rerailing ramps that were kept at various strategic locations.

The GWR had a total of twenty-seven small 0-4-0 tank engines at the time of the Grouping in 1923, thirteen from the Swansea Harbour Trust, nine from Messrs Powlesland a& Mason, two each from the Alexandra Docks and Taff Vale companies, and one from the Cardiff Railway. Fourteen survived into BR service and, of the three seen here, No 1140 was the first to go in 1958, followed by No 1144 in 1960 and finally 1152 in 1961.

This unusual image shows Fremington Quay, just west of Barnstaple on the line to Torrington and beyond. The engine running tender-first is a Bulleid 'Pacific' heading away from Barnstaple with a light load of just two coaches and a van. Such a large engine on a short train might appear unusual, but it was commonplace on the Southern lines west of Exeter, where the power available was useful during the summer months when loadings were far greater. Even so, there remains controversy as to whether this was the best use of available power; the Southern Region ending up with a total of 140 'home-grown' 'Pacifics', together with a few 'Britannia' Class engines in the 1950s. The question was simply what to do with them all, hence the cascade effect allowing older machines to be retired, although of course not all 140 were in service at any one time. Matters became ever more problematical after 1961 when electrification had covered Kent and steam was now concentrated on the Weymouth and Exeter lines together with some inter-regional workings from Brighton or Bournemouth. Even so, it was an excessive number of large engines and consequently withdrawals started in 1963, before a decision had been made as to whether diesel or electric power would replace them. In the event it was electrics, and the end of steam on the Southern came in 1967 to coincide with the Bournemouth electrification.

Meanwhile regional boundary changes meant that the lines west of Salisbury and all the former lines west of Exeter became the property of the Western Region, which was quick to realise why the term 'the withered arm' had been applied, there being little profit in operating any of them. Slowly each was closed – Ilfracombe, Padstow and Bude, and Exeter to Plymouth via Okehampton – leaving just stubs to Barnstaple and to Bere Alston for the remains of the Callington branch. As already mentioned, there is discussion, especially after the Dawlish floods, of reinstating the Plymouth route via Okehampton, and possibly returning to Wadebridge from Bodmin. Another group would like to see Ilfracombe reconnected by rail, but with the estuary bridge at Barnstaple long gone this could prove more problematical. We should not of course forget the former Lynton & Barnstaple narrow-gauge line, closed by the Southern back in 1935 but now energetically being rebuilt; indeed, one day we might see narrow-gauge trains restored on that particular route.

The modern Western Region is represented by 'Western' diesel No D1035 *Western Yeoman*, recorded at Subway Junction just outside Paddington. The 'Westerns' were the ultimate diesel-hydraulic class introduced by the WR, with all seventy-four named, each with the prefix 'Western'. With two 1,350hp engines installed they were intended to take the heaviest passenger trains on accelerated schedules, which had previously led to the uneconomic practice of double-headed diesels. Unfortunately in practice the hydraulic transmission came with as many disadvantages as advantages. On the plus side was the lower weight that was possible, but against this were the power losses involved in the transmission, resulting in a higher fuel consumption than had been anticipated. One positive point was reliability – if one engine failed it was possible to continue the journey, albeit hardly keeping to the schedule.

While the engines certainly had 'grunt', the top gear ratio had not been thought out and was too high, resulting in difficulty in reaching the claimed 90mph except when assistance was available from gravity – i.e. a downhill grade. This was no better than a 'Castle', although the diesel was capable of better acceleration and in maintaining a constant speed. Despite the last of the class being introduced in 1964, just a short time later the restrictions associated with the design were showing. They were incapable of achieving the faster speeds considered necessary to take on competition from the new M4 motorway and were also only fitted for steam heating, so could not work during the winter with the more modern Mk 2 coaches then coming into service, which were all electrically heated. BR was also seeking a standardised fleet, but the 'Westerns' and diesel-hydraulic types generally just did not fit in. The writing was on the wall, and all had been retired by the end of the 1970s.

The last few were often to be seen working heavy stone trains out of Merehead Quarry in Somerset, a type of duty for which they had never been designed. On such workings they were literally running on full power from the off, and no machine could take such punishment for long, so when one failed, especially if it was a major issue, it was simply cast aside and probably never repaired. This lack of reliability on such workings would later lead Foster Yeoman to purchase its own fleet – BR's motive power offerings were simply incapable or unreliable. However, the 'Westerns' did achieve cult status and no fewer than seven have been preserved, although not all are in operational condition. This cult status is hardly surprising, as at the time, and indeed since, they were regarded as one of the most aesthetically pleasing diesel types ever to operate on BR.

Our final Southern view – well, a Southern station but a Western train! – is at Launceston, mentioned earlier and looking towards Wadebridge. On the left is the former GWR station, and between the two the joint signal box with its two lever frames, one on each side, controlling the two routes but worked by one signalman. The lady on the left seems in a bit of a hurry, but she need not be concerned as the train – a GWR '55xx' and two Collett coaches – cannot depart until the starting signal has been raised. Again notice the station facilities, and consider the maintenance and, most importantly, the paucity of traffic, explaining why, although as an individual he is perhaps still blamed for the closure programme of the 1960s, a 'Dr Beeching' figure was inevitable. The railways had competition by this time, and a growing affluence in society meant that individuals sought their own independent means of transportation, 'door to door' rather than via a railway station (*never* a 'train station'!), followed by what might be a long walk to and from their ultimate destination.

The ash, coal and grease between the sleepers on the right-hand line in the foreground shows where the engines of trains stood, convenient for the water column. There is no parcels traffic, but the station gardens appear well kept – there was plenty of time to tend to such duties. Indeed, lack of traffic would invariably lead to good timekeeping.

For many years there have been no trains to Launceston, which went from two stations to one, then to none. Probably the replacement bus service has been similarly curtailed. So the wheel has turned almost full circle – little public transport, with the individual instead making his or her own way – but whereas once it was the horse and cart nowadays it is the car and motor lorry. Personally I would still prefer the '55xx'.

THE ARCHIVE

For the very last view in this work we return one last time to Plymouth. It is July 1961 and we are at Laira – 'the lair of the Kings' as it has been described – and indeed No 6026 *King John* is being coaled and made ready for its next working, which we can say without doubt will be east back to Paddington. The 'King' Class were the heaviest engines operating on the GWR/WR and as such had a restricted route availability. The Western had a colour coding for engines and routes according to which could go where; light branch lines would be 'uncoloured', after which came 'yellow', then 'blue', 'red' and finally 'double red'. No 6026 was 'double red', while No 5572 alongside was 'yellow', so could run over all lines except those classified as 'uncoloured'. Usually a coloured disc corresponding with the restriction was painted on the cab side, and for good reason, as there could well be speed or weight limits at certain points. (Additional 'dotted red', 'dotted blue' and 'X' restrictions were added later.)

Both engines are in their final full year of service, although No 6026 would receive a 'Heavy General' repair at Swindon in September 1961 but would be taken out of service just twelve months later. It has also received a double chimney, so, with a willing fireman and decent coal could still perform as well as the diesels that would replace it. No 5572 is slightly younger than the 'King', having been built in 1929 compared with 1927. This, though, was not a guarantee of longevity, for it was laid aside earlier, in April 1962. Neither would pass to the preservationists – the era of steam on the Western Region and indeed British Railways generally was accelerating towards a close.

Index

General, including locomotives types and classes

'14xx' 41, 42, 118, 120
'15xx' 74, 99, 108, 160
'22xx' ('2251') 118, 120, 192
'43xx' ('73xx') 118, 187, 192
'44xx' 42
'45xx' 18, 74, 99, 143, 166, 173, 178, 180
'47xx' 169
'51xx' 121
'61xx' 75, 120, 200
'55xx' 93, 170, 193, 204, 205
'57xx' 40, 99, 144, 160, 189, 196
'58xx' 118
'64xx' 49, 85, 99, 144
'74xx' 99
'84xx' 99, 121
'97'xx 121

'A1' 25, 117
'A2' 117, 184
'A3' 27, 94, 100, 117, 184
'A4' 27, 82, 94, 100, 117, 184, 195
Adams 4-4-2T 90, 120, 165
'Austerity' 2-8-0 .... 43, 51, 119
Auto-working 85, 132, 144, 167

Battery locos 87
'B1' 2, 26, 105, 116, 136, 186, 194, 195
'B12' 110, 111, 136
'B17' 68, 195
'B17/2' 116
'B17/6' 195
'Black 5' 35, 84, 125, 140, 188
Brake vans 86, 126, 154, 175
Beattie 'Well Tank' 90, 115, 181
BR Class 4 2-6-4T 8, 129
BR Class 4 2-6-0 58
BR Class 5 4-6-0 .... 20, 60, 162
BR Class 6 'Clan' 69
BR Class 7 'Britannia' 10, 46, 64, 65, 77, 89, 102, 105, 127, 151, 163, 172, 177, 184, 195, 202

BR Class 9 2-10-0 .... 82, 152
Breakdown crane 58, 83, 149, 159
Brush Type 2 .... 27, 77, 112, 136, 184, 198
Bulleid 'Pacific' 32, 71, 72, 202

'C12' 83
Caledonian 0-4-4T 75, 125, 199
Camping coaches 44, 45, 120
'Castle' 7, 8, 56, 70, 92, 96, 99, 138, 154, 158, 161, 164, 172, 175
City of Truro 63
'County' 158
'Crab' 46

'D' (SECR) 159
'D1' (SR) 66
'D16/3' 28, 66, 111
Departmental locomotives 14, 94, 105, 129, 186, 187, 199
Diesel hydraulic types 9
Diesel multiple units 35, 59, 95, 101, 126, 127, 142, 150, 167, 186
Diesel railcars (GWR) 69, 83
Diesel shunters (LMS and BR) 28, 101, 147, 184
Diesel shunters (Drewry) 29, 77
'Duchess' 3, 75, 191
'Dukedog' 70, 154, 191

'E4' (LNER) 16, 17
EE Type 4 .... 83, 131
Electric units (BRE) 176
Electric units (LMS) 55
Electric units (SR) 88
Electric Sleet Locomotive 52

'F' (LT) 53
'F4' 153
Fairburn 2-6-4T 35, 129
Fire buckets (SDJR) 117
Fowler 2-6-2T 139

'Grange' 12, 57, 73, 92, 120, 130, 168, 169, 186

'H2' 'Atlantic' (LBSCR) 171
'Hall' 87, 91, 92, 145, 185

Ivatt Class 2 2-6-2T 19, 54, 113, 155

'J15' 38, 110, 122, 137, 166, 172, 175
'J19' 136
'J35' 130
'J39' 117
'J52' 79, 83
'J66' 187
Johnson 3F 62
'Jubilee' 19, 140, 191

'K1' 26, 182
'K2/2' 26
'K5' 194
'King' 13, 161, 205

'L1' (LNER) 37, 81
LMS 2P 60
LSWR '0415' 54, 120

'M7' 11, 88, 92, 103, 189
Macintosh '439' 0-4-4T 93
'Merchant Navy' 47, 72
Metropolitan electrics 14, 112
MR iF 104
MR '1252' 146

'N' (SR) 98
'N2' 148, 174, 197
'N7' 55, 117, 136
NE 0-6-0T 84
Narrow gauge 30, 31, 107, 113, 202
NB Type 2 .... 61, 109, 145, 157
NLR tank 124
Nunn, Ken 78

'O2' (SR) 24, 34, 80, 92, 96, 97, 113, 123, 155

'P' 179
Pannier tanks (LT) 79, 85, 95, 99, 108, 115, 120, 132, 144

'Patriot' 140, 191
Peckett (LT) 95, 106
Petrol locos 23, 108
'Princess' 14, 191
Pullman restaurant cars 10
Pull-push working 88, 103, 117

'Q1' 198

Ramsbottom 0-6-0ST 89, 129
Robinson 4-4-2T 58

S&D 2-8-0 67
SHT 0-4-0T 106, 201
Signals 19, 78, 118, 126, 131, 142, 150,
156, 180, 183, 189, 196
Simplex 23
Stanier 2-6-4T 28, 35, 84, 139
Snowploughs 18, 46, 48, 166

'T9' 33
'Terrier' 104, 114, 167, 171
Tramway engines 23, 29, 50, 57, 89, 123
Tyneside electric 21

Underground stock 72, 124, 176

'V2' 117, 184
Vale of Rheidol... 107

'Warship' (NB and Swindon) 9, 86, 92, 128,
134, 141, 142
'Warship' (Swindon) 'Western' 86
'Western' 203

'Y9' 39

Locations

Aberystwyth 107
Alloa 130
Audley End 64
Audley End Tunnel 169
Axminster 54, 120, 165

Bangor 35, 139
Barnham (Suffolk) 175
Beattock 75, 92
Bere Alston 32, 80, 117, 135, 155,
189, 191, 202
Black Carr Sidings East 119
Bodmin North 180, 181, 196
Brent 86, 92, 158
Brighton 114, 129, 167, 179, 199, 202
Broad Street 55, 124
Brockenhurst 33, 47, 103
Burton 62

Callington 80, 113, 117, 155, 189, 202
Cambridge 10, 16, 17, 66, 76, 81,
116, 127, 169, 175
Camden 14, 139, 162, 191
Carlisle Kingmoor 4, 46, 89
Chacewater 173, 178
Cheddington 51
Chelsfield 88
Cholsey 164
Clapham Junction 114, 171
Coldrennick Viaduct 85
Coltishall 106
Cowes 42, 97
Crewe 10, 14, 19, 23, 28, 46, 65,
89, 122, 129, 140

Danygraig 106
Derby 20, 28, 29, 35, 62, 68, 87,
94, 104, 129, 139
Devonport Junction 61, 108
Doublebois 40, 126, 183

Edenbridge Town 71

Fremington Quay 202
Hall Farm Junction 77
Harlech 192
Haverhill 16, 17
Hayling Island 114, 171
Higher Town Tunnel 178
Hither Green 71, 149, 199
Holloway 27

Inverness 10, 36, 68, 84, 92, 125,
130, 141, 188, 199
Ipswich 29, 77, 127, 151, 177

Keith 26, 84, 188
Kemp Town 167
Keyham 143, 144, 157
King's Cross 25, 27, 128, 148, 152,
162, 174, 184, 197
King's Cross Top Shed 94, 117
Kittybrewster 8, 26, 188
Kyle of Lochalsh 44, 126, 182

Laira Junction 13, 57, 130, 131, 158, 161
Launceston 18, 42, 75, 135, 167,
191, 196, 204
Lea Bridge.. 199
Liskeard 40, 85, 99, 126, 168, 186
Liverpool Street 6, 10, 37, 81, 89, 102, 116,
124, 151, 163, 176, 199
Looe 99, 186
Lostwithiel 41, 156
Lydford 98
Lymington Junction 103

Machynlleth 41, 50, 70, 170, 192
March 10, 28, 43, 76, 111, 122,
125, 130, 182
Marland 22
Marylebone 68, 114
Mary Tavy & Blackdown 18, 191
Meldon Viaduct 32
Midford 60, 90
Midhurst 88

Millwall 124	Plymouth Devonport 113	Swindon 8, 12, 20, 41, 61, 63, 70, 73, 86, 87,
Moorswater 99, 186	Plymouth Friary 11, 34, 96, 113	92, 107, 108, 120, 128, 134, 141,
Morar 44	Plymouth Laira 7, 8, 12, 13, 41, 42, 49, 92, 96,	152, 161, 168, 169, 172,
Mundesley-on-Sea 59	130, 145, 161, 169,	175, 192, 200, 205
Mutley 158	170, 186, 205	
Neasden 14, 52, 53, 73, 79, 95, 112		Takeley 38, 133
Newton Abbot 56, 120, 145, 167	Rayne 38	Thorpe Junction (Norwich) 94
Newcastle Central 21	Romford 146	Truro 41, 63, 73, 101, 120, 168, 178, 183, 193
Nine Elms 33, 66, 123, 159, 189	Royal Albert Bridge 91, 132, 142, 143	
Norwich 65, 106, 110, 113, 122,	Ryde Pier Head 123	Uffington 200
150, 151, 163, 175		Upper Bank 15
Norwich Thorpe 10, 65, 89, 102, 150	Saltash 19, 49, 91, 132, 141,	
Noel Green Goods Depot 83	142, 143, 144	Wadebridge 75, 90, 115, 180, 196, 202, 204
	Shanklin 24	Welshpool 30, 31
Old Oak Common 8, 75, 108, 120,	Shepton Mallet 67	Wenford Bridge 90, 115, 180, 181
152, 161, 199	Stewarts Lane 71, 73	Westbourne Park 68, 75
	Stratford 6, 10, 16, 23, 28, 29, 65, 66, 68, 77,	West Thurrock Junction 55, 78
Par 134, 156, 160, 173, 193	89, 105, 110, 117, 122, 124, 136,	Whitehill (LMR) 43
Penmaenpool 118	137, 147, 151, 153, 166, 172,	Whitwell & Reepham 113
Plympton 158, 185	176, 186, 194, 195, 199	
Poplar Docks 87	Subway Junction 203	Yelverton 18, 42, 48, 97, 135
Princetown 42, 48, 167		York 6, 63, 78, 100, 119,
		132, 159, 199